Financial Markets

Stocks, bonds, money markets; IPOS, auctions, trading (buying and selling), short selling, transaction costs, currencies; futures, options

Vol. 2

Thomas H. McInish, Ph.D.

James Upson, Ph.D.

Copyright © 2014 by

Thomas H. McInish

and

James Upson

All rights reserved. This includes the right to reproduce any portion of this book in any form.

ISBN-13: 978-1493591695

ISBN-10: 149359169X

First edition published in February 2014

Second edition published in January 2015

Printed in the United States of America

DEDICATION

McInish: To Margaret McInish,
and Sheun and Ashley Aluko, with all my love

Upson: To my wife and children, with all my love.

TABLE OF CONTENTS

PREFACE

CHAPTER ONE

EQUITIES 1

    1. Introduction 4

    2. Types of equities 5

    3. Equity investment vehicles 26

    4. Problems faced by international investors 35

    5. Summary 40

CHAPTER TWO

DEBT SECURITIES 47

    1. Introduction 52

    2. Risks faced by debt investors 52

    3. The term structure of interest rates 53

    4. Ratings 57

    5. Islamic banking 61

    6. Money markets 62

    7. Bonds 71

    8. Summary 79

CHAPTER THREE

QUANTITATIVE ANALYSIS OF DEBT SECURITIES — 87

1. Introduction — 88
2. Time value of money — 88
3. Current yield and yield-to-maturity — 94
4. Total realized compound yield — 96
5. Duration — 98
6. Summary — 102

CHAPTER FOUR

GLOBAL CURRENCY MARKETS (FOREIGN EXCHANGE) — 105

1. Introduction — 107
2. Foreign exchange markets — 107
3. Dealing in foreign exchange markets — 112
4. The time pattern of foreign exchange trading — 121
5. Summary — 122

PREFACE

This book is written for market professionals and students who seek knowledge concerning financial markets. We focus on all four types of financial products: equities (stocks and warrants), debt instruments (bond and money market instruments), foreign exchange, and derivatives. We believe that in today's financial environment everyone must have a basic understanding of each of these markets. More and more individual investors are managing their own retirement portfolios. Both individuals and institutions are investing across borders so that it is not wise to only consider foreign exchange in international finance books and courses.

Volume 2 focuses on understanding equities, debt, and foreign exchange. Chapter 1 describes the features of equities. Chapters 2 and 3 describe both the characteristics of debt instruments and the analysis of debt instruments, including the term structure, yield-to-maturity, total realized compound yield and duration. Chapter 4 describes foreign exchange markets. Foreign exchange has traditionally been neglected in studies of financial markets. Financial institutions have led the trend toward international investing. But recently the discount broker Charles Schwab introduced accounts that allow individual U.S. investors in trade securities in a dozen countries outside the U.S. in local currencies

Volume 1 comprises five chapters. Chapter 1 describes the ways that equities and debt are created, including initial public offerings, private placements, and auctions. All financial assets have certain characteristics in common. All four product types are traded in markets, and, fortunately, the ways in which they are traded are limited. Chapter 2 describes the various trading venues including exchanges and alternative trading systems and how trading is conducted such as in batch or call sessions and in continuous markets.

Chapter 3 explains the various types of transactions costs associated with trading financial assets. We cover both explicit transactions costs including commissions and implicit transactions costs such as the cost resulting from needing to execute an order quickly. Chapter 4 discusses a topic that is frequently overlooked—clearing and settlement. Clearing and settlement involve the exchange of the financial assets and funds that result from trading. Historically, this topic has not been considered important for domestic investors. But as investors invest globally they encounter a wider variety of clearing and settlement practices. Also, the risks involved in clearing and settlement are greater in some markets than in others. Hence, the authors believe that understanding of this topic is essential for today's finance professionals and individual investors.

Chapter 5 deals with the regulation of financial markets. The particular institutions that regulate each market vary from country to country. But countries are increasingly coordinating their regulation of financial markets. During the crisis of 2008 governments worldwide cooperated in instituting bans of short selling. And efforts to combat money laundering and other financial crimes now have a worldwide scope.

Volume 3 focuses on understanding options, futures, and swaps—financial products used by speculators and hedgers. This is not just a topic for speculators or sophisticated professionals. All investors need to understand these products. Derivatives can be used to protect portfolios and generate income, characteristics that may become more important as the population in developed countries around the world ages.

Hedging is another important concept related to derivatives. Hedging aims to reduce or eliminate risk due to fluctuations in the price of assets. We devote a chapter to this topic and put this chapter in Volume 3 because derivatives are the primary tools used in hedging.

Providing background for writing this book, the authors have traveled extensively, visiting exchanges, universities, brokerage firms, banks, and other businesses in many countries, including Argentina, Australia, Austria, Canada, Chile, China, Croatia, Denmark, England, Finland, France, Germany, Greece, Hong Kong, Italy, Indonesia, Japan, Malaysia, Mexico, Lithuania, Luxembourg, the Netherlands, New Zealand, Norway, the Philippines, Poland, Portugal, Russia, Singapore, Spain, Sweden, Switzerland, Taiwan, Thailand, Turkey, Viet Nam and the USA.

CHAPTER ONE

EQUITIES

Key Terms

12b-1 fee—a fee paid from the assets of a mutual fund to cover marketing expenses.

Accredited investor—a financial institution or individual meeting the requirements of SEC Rule 501 Regulation D that is eligible to purchase certain offerings not available to non-accredited investors.

Capped warrants—low exercise price warrants with the upside gain capped at a stated level.

Classified common stock—common stock that is divided into classes with different rights. Most commonly one class will have more votes per share than another class.

Closed-end investment company—a type of managed investment company that has a fixed number of shares outstanding and rarely raises new funds.

Convertible preferred—preferred stock that can be exchanged for another security, typically the common shares of the firm.

Country risk—risk due to the political and economic conditions in a particular country.

Covered warrant—a warrant for which the issuer is not the firm whose shares underlie the warrant.

Cumulative preferred—preferred stock for which the firm continues to have the obligation to pay any missed dividends.

Cumulative voting—a method of voting for corporate directors that gives each share a number of votes N equal to the number of directors to be elected and requiring votes to elect each individual directors. A shareholder owning N votes can elect one director.

Exchange-traded fund (ETF)—shares of beneficial interest in a unit trust owning a pool of underlying securities.

Floating rate preferred—preferred stock that has a dividend that is reset periodically.

Hedge fund—an investment organization whose management receives compensation in the form of performance incentives rather than based on the amount of assets held or the number of transactions made and that typically uses leverage in the execution of its investment strategies.

Index warrants—warrants with the payment at expiration linked to the value of an index such as the S&P 500 Index, the Nikkei Index and the FT-SE 100 Index.

Intrinsic value of a warrant—the difference between the cost of acquiring an asset by exercising a warrant and the market value of the asset acquired.

Load—a commission charged at the time of the purchase of an open-end investment company.

Low exercise price warrants—warrants with a low exercise price such as 0.01 AUD.

Managed investment companies—corporations whose primary business is investing in other firms and in which investors purchase shares that represent an undivided interest in the firm's assets.

Mutual fund—a type of open end investment company in the business of investing in financial assets. Investments can be initiated by buying shares directly from the mutual fund and liquidated by selling the shares back to the mutual fund.

Net asset value—the value of the assets owned by an investment company less its liabilities.

No load—a type of open-end investment company that does not charge a commission at the time of purchase or sale.

Open-end investment company—a type of managed investment company that is continuously issuing new shares.

Participating preferred—preferred stock that has a dividend that is based at least in part on the firm's earnings.

Poison pill—a provision in a firm's bylaws or charter that provide protection if anyone acquires a significant ownership in the firm without the approval of the board of directors.

Preferred stock—a type of equity or ownership of the firm that has a stated claim on the firm assets and earnings but that cannot force the bankruptcy of the firm if it is unable to pay.

Preemptive rights—the right to participate in new equity offerings on a pro rata basis.

Premium (for warrants)—the difference between the market price of a warrant and its value if exercised immediately. (Note that there are a number of other definitions of this term in finance that apply to other types of securities.)

Publicly traded investment companies—same as closed-end investment company.

Pyramid—a method of corporate control in which individuals can control firms by owning a partial but controlling interest in one firm with a partial but controlling interest in another firm and so forth.

Rear-end load—a commission charged at the time of the sale of an open-end investment company.

Right—a security distributed pro rata to existing equity owners that allows the purchase of additional equity at a specified subscription price prior to a specified expiration time.

Short sale—the sale of an asset in the hopes of buying it back later at a lower price.

Unit trusts—a type of managed investment company formed by a deed of trust between a trustee and an investment manager under which the investment manager will purchase securities for the beneficial interest of the unit holders who own a pro rata interest in the trust assets.

Unit investment trust—a fixed pool of securities in which each investor has an interest proportionate to their contribution.

> IN THIS CHAPTER, we describe the basic features of common and preferred stock. Then, we discuss three important types of equity issues:
> - Depository receipts for investors investing in non-domestic stocks,
> - Warrants, and
> - Rights offerings
>
> Next, we describe in detail a common way of managing investment portfolios, namely:
> - Pooled investment plans.
>
> Finally, we consider problems faced by international investors, especially:
> - Restrictions on foreign ownership

1. Introduction

The creation of new securities takes place in the **primary market**, the market for the initial sale of securities. We describe how these securities are created in this chapter. A hallmark of the primary market is that the proceeds from the sale of securities go to the issuer of the securities.

The aggregate value of world equity markets is in the trillions of USDs. There has been extraordinary development of equity markets in the 1990s. Table 1-1 shows the 10 largest exchanges in terms of the USD capitalization of domestic listings. In some cases market value of listings may not fully reflect differences in size. Some exchanges allow trading in unlisted securities. Also, cross-holdings, the holding of stock in one listed-company by another listed company, are common in some countries and rare in others. Cross holdings inflate the value of listings when measured in terms of market value of outstanding shares. Failure to account for cross holdings would overstate the value of equities on the Oslo Stock Exchange by 20%. Financial leverage and the aggregate return of the listed equities would also be significantly understated (See Bohren and Michalsen 1994)).

Table 1-1. Largest equity markets by capitalization

		Bill. USD End 2012	% Change from 2011
1	NYSE Euronext (US)	14,086	19.4
2	NASDAQ OMX (US)	4,582	19.2
3	Tokyo Stock Exchange Group	3,479	4.6
4	London Stock Exchange Group	3,397	4.0
5	NYSE Euronext (Europe)	2,832	15.8
6	Hong Kong Exchanges	2,832	25.4
7	Shanghai SE	2,547	8.1
8	TMX Group	2,059	7.7
9	Deutsche Börse	1,486	25.5
10	Australian SE	1,387	15.7

Source: World Federation of Exchanges, 2012 WFE Market Highlights, January 2013.

As a percentage of Gross Domestic Product (GDP), stock market capitalization in Chile, Hong Kong, Malaysia, and Singapore have been comparable to, or even exceeded, that of the United States and United Kingdom. In many emerging markets, stock markets have played a more important role in raising capital for industry than in most industrialized countries. According to Robert Shakotko, manager of the emerging-markets database at the International Financial Corp., the World Bank's private finance vehicle, "With the advent of money that crosses national boundaries very quickly, it's become more important . . . to have a functioning exchange and attract foreign money."[1]

2. Types of equities

2.1. Common stock

Common stockholders are the owners of the firm. The common stockholders have the right to receive all of the assets and earnings of the firm after the obligations of other equity and debt holders have been met.

---

[1] Vogel, Thomas T, Jr., Exchanges sprout in developing nations, Wall Street Journal, November 14, 1995, p. C1.

In the U.S. common stockholders usually have the exclusive right to elect the board of directors. In some countries, e.g. Germany, other stakeholders such as employees, have a right to elect directors. In most cases each share of common stock has one vote and a majority of the votes cast is required to elect all of the directors. Shareholder votes are often required on major corporate decisions such as mergers. Companies have devised a number of ways to make it more difficult for stockholders to change the board of directors. The terms of the board members may be staggered so that only a few are elected each year. Stockholders have to wait for several years before a majority of the board can be changed. There might be classified common stock with some classes having more votes than other classes. The class A shares might have 1 vote each and the class B shares 10 votes each. Hence, an investor or group of investors might be able to maintain control of the firm without having enough resources to own a majority of the shares.

One study examines the ownership structure of large corporation in 27 wealthy countries and finds that very few of these firms are widely owned. Instead, they are mostly controlled by families.[1] Controlling shareholders typically have much more control than would be indicated simply by their claims on the cash flows of the firm. This power can be accomplished by **pyramid** ownership structures in which there is a partial but controlling interest in one firm with a partial but controlling interest in another firm and so forth. A second source of power is through participation in management. In the U.S. managerial ownership for a group of publicly-held companies has increased from 13 percent in 1935 to 21 percent in 1995.[2]

The U.S. and some other countries, particularly common law countries, have significant protection for minority shareholders. It has recently become popular for companies to have **poison pills**, provisions in their bylaws or charter that provide protection if anyone acquires a significant ownership in the firm without the approval of the board of directors. The pill might provide that all of the existing shareholders other than the new holder have the right to purchase equity in the firm at a very cheap price. Such a provision makes it prohibitively expensive for outsiders to gain control of the firm. Historically, in the U.S. common stockholders have had

---

[1] Lopez de Silanes, La Porta, and Shleifer (1999).
[2] Holderness, Kroszner, and Sheehan (1999).

preemptive rights—the right to participate in new equity offerings on a pro rata basis. This provision was designed to prevent the dilution of stockholders' ownership percentage. Now preemptive rights are typically eliminated in firm charters.

Rather than one share one vote, some firms use a voting method called **cumulative voting**. In this method each shareholder can cast as many votes as they own shares times the number of candidates. Each shareholder's votes can be divided in any way so that if n directors are being elected a shareholder who owns 1/n of the shares can be assured of electing one director if all of that shareholders' votes are cast for a single director. Suppose that a firm has 100 shares outstanding and is electing five directors. The number of votes that can be cast is (5 X 100 =) 500 and it takes at least 100 votes to win a directorship. Hence, a shareholder owning 20 shares can elect a director. Cumulative voting is in contrast to the typical cases in which shareholders who own a majority of the shares can elect all of the directors.

2.2. Preferred stock

Preferred stock is equity. Preferred stockholders often have a claim to a stated dividend and stated assets in the event of the liquidation of the firm. But the preferred stockholders cannot force the bankruptcy of the firm if the stated dividend obligations are not met. In some cases preferred stockholders gain extra rights such as the right to vote for directors or even to elect a majority of directors if the firm fails to meet its obligations to the preferred holders. The firm may be prohibited from paying dividends on common stock if its obligations to the preferred holders have not been met. For **cumulative preferred** the firm has an obligation to pay any missed dividends before paying any dividends to the common stockholders. **Participating preferred** does not have an entirely fixed dividend, but instead its dividend is based at least in part on the earnings of the firm. **Convertible preferred** may be exchanged for another security, typically the common shares of the firm. **Floating rate preferred** has a dividend payment that is reset periodically. The reset rate may be based on some capital market rate such as LIBOR or in some cases a Dutch auction is used to reset the rate.

Firms that have regulatory obligations to maintain certain levels of equity such as banks and brokerage firms may find preferred stock useful. Also, in the U.S. preferred stock has some tax advantages in that corporate recipients of preferred stock dividends typically pay a lower U.S. Federal income tax rate on these dividends (dividends on common equity receive similar treatment).

2.3. Depository receipts

A DR is a negotiable certificate issued by a depository bank such as J.P. Morgan or the Bank of New York. J.P. Morgan created the American Depository Receipt (ADR) in 1927 to simplify investment in non-U.S. companies by U.S. investors. Sometimes the term Global Depository Receipts (GDR) is used for marketing reasons or to indicate an issue being sold in several countries, but GDRs and ADRs sold in the U.S. are identical. Here we call both Depository Receipts (DR). Since the DR is considered to be a U.S. security, it can be freely traded in the U.S. and is the same as other U.S. securities for purposes of clearing and settlement. Therefore, DRs typically make it easier and cheaper to trade non-U.S. securities in the U.S. There are DRs traded on the New York and American Stock Exchanges, on NASDAQ, and over-the-counter. In the U.S. there are over 900 DR programs with issuers from more than 40 countries. Figure 1-1 shows the number of ADRs per country in 2013.[1]

Moreover, many countries throughout the world now have their own version of DRs. In September 1995 Unocal Corp. signed a depository agreement and became the first U.S. Fortune 500 company to have its depository receipts listed on the Stock Exchange of Singapore. One interesting aspect of the agreement is that the DRs traded in USD rather than in SGD, which may account for its low trading volume.

DRs are created and destroyed at will. The depository bank arranges for a bank in the issuer's home country to serve as the local custodian. The bank

---

[1] ADR web sites include those of J.P. Morgan, http://www.adr.com/, the Bank of New York, http://www.bankofny.com/bus/Biisadr.htm and Deutsche Morgan Grenfell, http://www.adr-dmg.com/deposit.htm.

may establish the DR program unilaterally or with the consent and support of the issuing firm.

Figure 1-1. Number of ADRs for selected countries

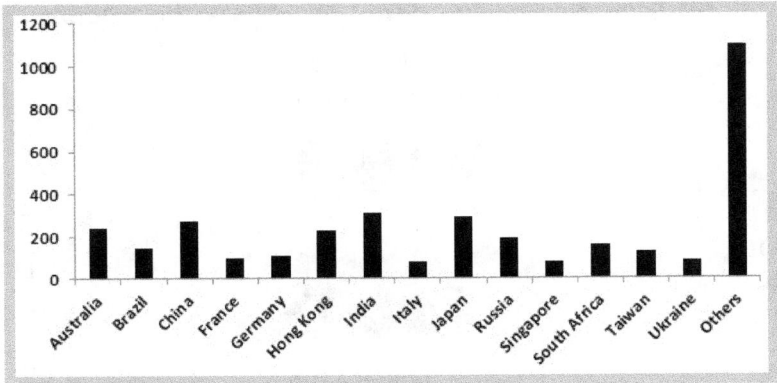

Source: Constructed by authors based on data from J.P. Morgan web sites.

Figure 1-2 presents a schematic of the process by which the DRs are created and destroyed after the program has begun. In the U.S. a non-U.S. owner of the shares may deliver them to the custodial bank to have DRs created for sale in the U.S. market. Or a U.S. broker, acting for a U.S. client, may purchase shares in the home market, through an affiliate or another brokerage firm, convert the USDs received from its client into the currency needed to pay for the shares, and deliver the shares to the custodial bank. On the same day that the custodial bank receives the shares, the bank notifies the depository bank, which then issues the DRs and delivers them to the broker for redelivery to their client. The DRs may be canceled through a process that reverses the previous steps or a DR holder may simply take possession of the underlying shares. The ability to create and destroy ADRs keeps the prices of the underlying shares and the receipts close together through arbitrage.

There are four levels of DRs in the U.S., differing primarily in the amount of information provided to investors and the consequent access granted to U.S. markets. Level-III DRs require additional paperwork, but allow the issuance and sale of new shares to raise equity U.S. capital markets. Unsponsored DRs are issued by depositories in response to market demand. In the past there was no issuer involvement, but today the issuer must sign certain documents. Sponsored Level-I DRs do not require

Figure 1-2. Creating and destroying ADRs

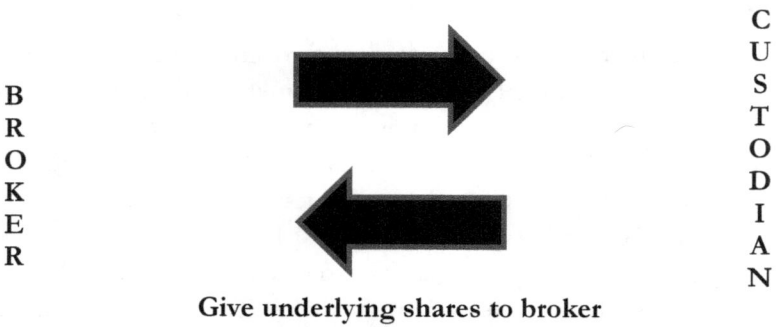

Source: Prepared by authors.

compliance with U.S. GAAP or disclosure beyond that required in the home country. Level-I DRs can be traded in the U.S. over-the-counter market and on some non-U.S. exchanges. Level-II DRs can be traded on a U.S. exchange, but require financial statements conforming to U.S.

requirements. In addition to the three levels of sponsored programs, companies can use U.S. capital markets to raise funds through a sale of sponsored DRs to institutional buyers in a private placement. It usually costs less than 10,000 USD to establish a Level-I program and about 75,000 USD to establish a Level-II program.

From the point of view of the issuer, DRs can:

Increase the market for the issue,

Enhance the image of the company in the international market,

Provide a means for raising new equity capital and serve as a vehicle for acquisitions, and

Allow employees to invest in the parent company.

A number of active money managers prefer direct investment in the home market rather than the use of DRs. But for smaller institutions, cost, market access issues, and global custody problems may lead to a preference for DRs. Depending on the country in which the DR is issued and the particular arrangements, the advantages of DR programs to investors may include one or more of the following:

1. DRs are traded in the local market and the clearing and settlement process is the same as for local securities.

2. DRs are often quoted in local currency.

3. The depository bank arranges the conversion of dividends into local currency at competitive rates.

4. DRs overcome many obstacles to institutional investment outside the home country.

5. DRs sometimes reduce transfer taxes.

6. Whereas actual certificates may be in bearer form in some countries, in the U.S. DRs are registered certificates, providing a record of ownership in case of loss.

DRs may reduce legal problems from countries that claim jurisdiction over the estate of a deceased owner.

DRs may offer an efficacious way of attaining international exposure and diversification. Adding as few as seven DRs to a portfolio comprising the U.S. Standard and Poor's 500 substantially reduces the risk of the portfolio.[1]

---

[1] Wahab and Khandwala (1993).

2.4. Warrants

A warrant is a security giving the owner a claim to an asset at a specified price before a specified time. The specified price is the exercise price and the specified time is the expiration date. Traditionally, warrants have given the right to purchase an equity interest in the issuer at the exercise price. If the warrant gives the right to purchase an asset, the **intrinsic value** of a warrant is the difference between the cost of acquiring the asset by exercising the warrant and the market value of the asset. The difference between the market price of a warrant and its intrinsic value is the **premium**.

Warrants have been issued in most financial markets including those of Austria, Brazil, Germany, India, Italy, Japan, Korea, Malaysia, Mexico, Singapore, Switzerland, Thailand, the United Kingdom, and the United States. The large number of European warrants outstanding is testified to by the European Warrant Fund Inc., traded on the NYSE, which invests primarily in equity warrants, index warrants, covered warrants and long term options of European issuers. Historically, most warrants have been issued along with other securities such as common stock (in units) or (attached to) bonds. Typically, after the issue has been sold the warrants trade separately from the bonds of stock. In some cases, if a bond and warrant are sold together the bond can be used as payment, typically at face value.

An offering of warrants and stock together may attract investors who are more speculatively minded. Since, as we indicated, the common stock and warrants will usually trade separately, the company may attract demand both from equity investors and derivative investors. Further, if the firm is not able to raise all of the capital it wants at one time, an appropriately priced warrant issue may give a reasonable prospect of obtaining more funds later. Hindalco Industries issued 4,473 million units, each comprising two shares and one warrant to purchase an additional share. The combination of a common stock and warrant offering is common for some types of financial firms in the international markets such as the U.K.

There are many variations in the terms of warrants. The U.S. investment company, TriContinental Corporation, has warrants outstanding that do not have an expiration date. In 1991 Eurotunnel issued a warrant permitting exercise when certain financial conditions were met. Danae Investment Trust warrants expire when the affairs of the trust are wound up and The Hong Kong Investment Trust warrants expired 30 days after the 1995 annual report was issued. Occasionally, firms unilaterally extend the life of their warrants. This has posed a problem for investors in the U.S. who had developed strategies of shorting expiring warrants (recall that a short sale is the sale of an asset in the hopes of buying it back later at a lower price). In the U.S. some warrant issues have had provisions allowing the company to force exercise. Some warrants contain provisions that allow the firm to make adjustments to prevent the warrant from expiring worthless. Sometimes the company can convert an out-of-the-money warrant into a small amount of common stock or lower the exercise price so that the warrant's intrinsic value is positive.

The Australian Stock Exchange lists a number of warrants with unusual features. Most of these warrants can only be exercised at maturity. **Low exercise price warrants** are similar to equity warrants except that the exercise price is 0.01 AUD. **Capped warrants** are low exercise price warrants with the upside gain capped at a stated level. **Index warrants** link the payment at expiration to the value of an index such as the S&P 500 Index, the Nikkei Index and the FT-SE 100 Index.

The issuance of warrants on a stand-alone basis without accompanying securities is less common. In a few cases warrants have been issued alone either as a way to raise equity capital or, more commonly, as a form of compensation. The U.K. firm Hanson used warrants as part of the payment in two takeovers. In the first instance, Hanson acquired Consolidated Gold Fields for a combination of cash and warrants. Then, Hanson offered identical warrants as part of the acquisition price of Beazer.

The International Finance Corporation issued 1,000,000 Asia Tiger 100™ Index Call Warrants through the investment banking firm of CIBC Oppenheimer. Upon expiration in November 2002 the owner received an amount based on the increase in value of the index over the initial value. These warrants were traded on the Chicago Board Options Exchange.[1]

---

[1] The Chicago Board of Trade also lists several other similar products, which can be reviewed at: http://www.cboe.com/products/prodspec/txs-spec.htm.

While single company warrants most commonly allow for the purchase of an equity interest in the issuer, sometimes the warrant allows for the purchase of an equity interest in another firm. In 1983 Dart and Kraft Finance issued a warrant allowing the purchase of shares of Minnesota Mining and Manufacturing, a firm in which Dart and Kraft held an equity stake. Sometimes, the exercise price of a warrant may change during the life of the warrant. Asahi Glass, a Japanese company, issued warrants that allowed the holder to purchase its common stock at a fixed price in USD. Therefore, this warrant changes value in response both to changes in the value of Asahi common stock and changes in the USD/JPY exchange rate.

A growing phenomenon, especially in Europe, is the issuance of **covered warrants**. The principal difference between a covered warrant and other warrants is that the issuer is not the firm whose securities underlie the warrant, or even another firm that acquired shares in the subject firm in the past. Instead, the issuer is an investment banker that acquires the shares for the express purpose of issuing the warrant. At first, the warrants were for shares of Japanese companies. Both Morgan Stanley and Baring Brothers have issued covered warrants on the shares of Fuji Fire and Marine. The success of the market for Japanese covered warrants has led to growth in the number of issuers and the types of warrants issued. 171 covered warrants were launched when the London Stock Exchange began trading these products in 2002. SG Warburg OTC issued a covered warrant with shares of the European firm, Phillips, as the underlying asset. Barclays de ZoeteWedd Warrants have the American Depository shares of the Mexican company, Telmex, as the underlying asset. Goldman Sachs has issued covered warrants on individual companies in a wide range of countries including Belgium, Germany, Finland, France, Hong Kong, Russia, the Netherlands, Italy, Sweden, Spain, Switzerland, the UK, and the US.[1]

A distinctive feature of the covered warrant market is the many issues of basket covered warrants. These are warrants that allow the purchase or, sometimes, the sale, of a basket of stocks at a fixed price until expiration. Some basket covered warrants are for particular countries, some for particular industries, and some for particular regions. Morgan Stanley's

---

[1] For information about Goldman Sachs warrants see: http://www.gs.com/warrants/main.ggi/english.

Argentine blue chip basket allows the purchase of shares in five firms (weights): YPF ADR, 32.80%; Telefonica ADR, 32.20%; Galicia ADR, 14.20%; Frances ADR, 12.80%; and BAESA ADR, 8.00%. Kidder Peabody International's U.S. insurance basket comprised equal proportions of American Insurance, USF & G, Chubb, General Re Corp., and Marsh & McLennan. The warrants expired May 31, 1996 and were exercisable in USD. Four million warrants were issued, half in USD and half in CHF. Morgan Stanley's Eastern European exposure basket covered holdings in nine firms with weights ranging from 6.6% to 15.9%. Goldman Sachs has issued covered warrants for baskets of stocks in various countries including internet stocks in the US.

2.5. Rights offering

The purpose of a rights offering is to raise new equity capital. We have previously explored several ways that firms can raise additional equity capital including retained earnings, new offerings of stock to the public (the first offering is called an "initial public offering" or IPO and subsequent issues are called seasoned equity offerings (SEOs), and warrants. In recent years almost half of the equity in Canada has been raised through rights offers.[1] It is also a popular method in many European countries such as the United Kingdom[2] and in Japan. But while rights offerings were also used frequently in the U.S. until the 1970s, they are now rarely used.[3]

For each year, 1975-2011, Table 1-2 shows the number of rights offerings and the proportion of total offerings by number for U.S. and Japanese firms. In the U.S. the use of rights offerings for NYSE- or AMEX-listed firms disappeared after 1981, but in Japan right offerings continued for several more years, dying out slowly in the 21st century. Descriptive

---

[1] See Eckbo and Verma, 1994.
[2] See Marsh, 1979; Loderer and Zimmerman, 1988.
[3] Gabelli Funds, Inc. provides a description of rights offerings and a discussion of its own rights offerings at:
http://www.gabelli.com/Gab_phtml/basics.html. Safeguard Scientifics, Inc. monitors US rights offerings and provides information at: http://www.safeguard.com/ro.html.

characteristics for Japanese firms using rights and public offerings are presented in Table 1-2. Several relationships are noteworthy. Note the larger size of the rights issue in relation to a public offering.

2.5.1. How rights offerings work

Before explaining why firms use rights offerings we explain how rights offerings work. A right is a security distributed pro rata to existing equity owner that allows the purchase of additional equity at a specified subscription price before a specified expiration time. The firm is free to set the subscription price at any level. If the subscription price is below the market price at the expiration date, holders of the rights must exercise or the rights expire worthless, resulting in a loss of their value to the holder. Rights are distributed to the current holders of equity as a dividend with the owner of each share receiving one or more rights. Typically, if the original owner of a right does not wish to exercise, the right can be sold to another investor before their expiration. The time between the issuance of the rights and their expiration is usually short and may amount to only a few weeks. Naturally, the stock price of the firm issuing the rights is likely to fluctuate during the period during which the rights are outstanding. The lower the subscription price is set compared with the current stock price the more likely the stock price will be greater than the subscription price at expiration and that the rights will be exercised. Rights will only be exercised if the market price of the stock is above the exercise price, especially at the time of expiration. If the current market price of the shares is 10 USD, a subscription price of 5 USD is more likely to result in the right being exercised than a subscription price of 9.5 USD. In the latter case, the market price is more likely to decline below the subscription price. Since the purpose of a rights offering is to raise new equity, the firm desires that the rights be exercised.

Rights offerings do not change the value of the firm (except by the amount of new capital raised). Otherwise, firms could forget their operations and simply create value by issuing rights. This observation is an affirmation of Modigliani-Miller Proposition I, which says that "the market

Table 1-2. Rights offerings in the U.S. and Japan, 1975-1991.
The number of rights offerings and the proportion that these represent of the combined total of rights and public offerings (in parentheses) is shown. No rights offerings are reported for the U.S. sample after 1981.

	Japan		Japan	U.S.
Year	Offerings	Year	Offerings	Offerings
1975	166 (0.582)			10 (0.11)
1976	102 (0.526)			5 (0.05)
1977	120 (0.296)			3 (0.05)
1978	66 (0.211)			4 (0.04)
1979	54 (0.166)			4 (0.05)
1980	34 (0.121)			5 (0.03)
1981	67 (0.199)			3 (0.02)
1982	45 (0.165)	1997	9 (0.063)	
1983	18 (0.137)	1998	1 (0.077)	
1984	23 (0.111)	1900	0	
1985	40 (0.173)	2000	2 (0.052)	
1986	27 (0.115)	2001	3 (0.149)	
1987	26 (0.067)	2002	0	
1988	40 (0.075)	2003	3 (0.070)	
1989	32 (0.045)	2004	4 (0.048)	
1990	39 (0.067)	2005	3 (0.036)	
1991	40 (0.101)	2006	0	
1992	20 (0.116)	2007	1 (0.014)	
1993	9 (0.043)	2008	1 (0.033)	
1994	2 (0.010)	2009	1 (0.019)	
1995	12 (0.076)	2010	1 (0.083)	
1996	9 (0.035)	2011	0	

Source: The Japanese data are taken from the Tokyo Stock Exchange Fact Book 2012 and the U.S. data, which are for American and New York Stock Exchange-listed firms, are derived from Eckbo and Masulis (1992).

value of any firm is independent of its capital structure and is given by capitalizing its expected return at the rate ... appropriate to its risk class."[1]

---

[1] Modigliani and Miller (1958, p. 268).

Ceteris paribus, the value of the firm is increased by the amount of money raised in the rights offering. We can study rights offerings considering the whole firm or an individual portfolio. We will use the individual portfolio.

Define the following terms:

n = the number of shares of a firm's stock in a portfolio before the rights offering, and

P_0 = the firm's stock price before the rights offering.

The value of the portfolio prior to the rights offering is:

$$nP_0$$

We are interested in calculating the theoretical value of each share after the rights offering and the theoretical trading price of each right.

To determine the theoretical value of each share after the rights offering we need to determine how much new money the firm obtains when the rights are exercised and how many new shares are issued. Let

q = the number of new shares received if all of the portfolio's rights are exercised,

P_c = the total cost of one new share, and

P_r = the cost of buying one shares in the rights offering.

We assume that all of the rights are exercised. The value of the portfolio after the rights offering is:

$$nP_0 + qP_c$$

The number of shares held in the portfolio after the rights offering is:

$$n + q$$

Therefore, the theoretical value of each share after the rights offering is:

$$(nP_0 + qP_c)/(n + q) \qquad 1.1$$

If one right entitles the holder to purchase one share the value of each right is:

$$(nP_0 + qP_c)/(n + q) - P_r \qquad 1.2$$

If a firm wants to allow shareholders to purchase say 2 shares for each share currently held, the firm can distribute two rights per share, each entitling the holder to buy one new share. Alternately, if the right entitles the owner to buy less than a whole share then the values in equation 1.2 need to be reduced proportionally. So assume that each right allows the owner to buy only on-half share. Then the values in equation 1.2 need to be multiplied by 0.5.

We now consider three hypothetical cases. We wish to find the values of equations 1.1 and 1.2 for each case. Let $n = 100$ and $P_0 = 10$ USD. The value of this portfolio prior to a right offering is:

$$nP_0 = 10 \times 100 = 1{,}000 \text{ USD}$$

Case 1: Let $P_c = 6$ USD, and $q = 100$. Evaluating equation 1.1 gives:

$$((100 \times 10 \text{ USD}) + (100 \times 6 \text{ USD}))/(100 + 100) = 8 \text{ USD}$$

Evaluating equation 1.2 gives:

8 USD – 6 USD = 2 USD

Case 2: Let $P_c = 6$ USD, and $q = 200$. Evaluating equation 1.1 gives:
$((100 \times 10 \text{ USD}) + (200 \times 6 \text{ USD}))/((100 + 200)) = 7.33$ USD
Evaluating equation 1.2 gives:
7.33 USD – 6 USD = 1.33 USD
Case 3: Let $P_c = 6$ USD, and $q = 50$. Evaluating equation 1.1 gives:
$((100 \times 10 \text{ USD}) + (50 \times 6 \text{ USD}))/((100 + 50)) = 8.67$ USD
Evaluating equation 1.2 gives:
0.5(8.67 USD – 6 USD) = 1.33 USD

It might be useful to consider a real example chosen because it is unusual and provides an interesting illustration. On May 21, 1986 Brock Hotel Corporation of Dallas, Texas, distributed 20 rights for each share of its common stock. Each right entitled the holder to purchase one share of common stock before expiration of the rights on June 6, 1986, at an exercise price of 0.15 USD. At the close of trading on May 20, 1986, Brock was trading at 20/32 (0.625) USD. Since the value of the stock was 0.625 USD just before the rights distribution, the projected value of the stock/rights portfolio, if the rights were exercised and the value of the stock did not change is 0.625 USD + (20 × 0.15USD) = 3.625. Therefore, the projected value of each post-rights share is 3.625 USD/21 = 0.1726 USD and the projected value of a right is 0.1726 - 0.15 = 0.0226 USD. At the close of trading on May 22, 1986 (the first day of trading for the rights), the stock closed at 0.1875 USD, slightly higher than its projected value of 0.1726. Since the stock was worth more than projected, the right should also be worth more. Specifically, the right should be worth 0.1875 - .15 = 0.0375 USD. In fact, the right closed at 0.03125. Another way to look at this is that following the distribution of the rights the owner of one pre-rights share owned one share of stock and 20 rights for a total value of 0.1875 + (20 X 0.03125) = 0.8125, so that the value of the stock/rights portfolio had increased slightly. In any event, the actual values of the stock and rights conform very well to their projected values, especially considering that due to the U.S. convention in effect at the time of trading only in ticks of 1/64, 1/32, 1/16, 1/8, etc., not all theoretical values were attainable.

Since firms set the subscription price, naturally, they set it at a level that is low enough to make the likelihood of success high. But a substantial price decline can result in an unsuccessful offering. Therefore, many firms using rights offerings hire an investment banker who agrees to exercise any rights that are not exercised by the firm's stockholders. In this way, the success of the offering is guaranteed, but, of course, a fee must be paid to the underwriter. The potential usefulness of standby underwriting is illustrated by the case of Cheung Kong Group that announced a rights offering at a substantial discount to the market price just before the stock market crash of October 1987. Following the crash the price of Cheung Kong Group stock fell well below the subscription price. The shareholders did not exercise their rights forcing the underwriters to honor their commitment to buy a substantial number of shares at the exercise price. In 1991 Time Warner announced that it would raise new equity using a rights offering. If all rights were exercised the offering price was 105 USD, but the offering price was scaled down if only part of the rights were exercised. If only 60% were exercised the price was 63 USD. On June 3, 1991, Time Warner stock sold for 119.125 USD, but thereafter the stock's price declined to less than 100 USD per share. Hence, to decide whether or not to exercise a shareholder had to guess what other shareholders would do. Time Warner was forced to abandon its variable-price rights offering. Subsequently, the firm completed a conventional rights offering.[1]

In Norway seasoned equity issues on the Oslo Stock Exchange now take place almost exclusively through the use of underwritten rights offerings.[2] The market response to rights offerings that are not underwritten is significantly positive. Those that are underwritten elicit the least favorable response most likely because they are more expensive and also because the expected takeup of shares by current shareholders is likely related to the profitability of the investments to be undertaken with the funds raised.

In November, 2011, a large Italian bank, UniCredit, announced that it intended to have a rights offering to raise 7.5 billion EUR. Prices for the bank's shares over the period of the offering were are given in Table 1-3. A group of banks, including Bank of America, served as standby underwriters who would purchase the shares that shareholders did not take up. UniCredit's share price declined from 8.32 EUR in November to 5.41 EUR when the rights offering began. Each shareholder received 1 right for each share held and each right entitled the holder to purchase one new share at 1.943 EUR. Immediately after the right offering the price of UniCredit's share fell substantially and there were fears that the rights offering would fail. But the price subsequently rallied and the offering was successful.

2.5.2. Factors influencing the choice of rights versus public offerings

The use of rights offerings avoids all or part of the substantial fees charged by investment bankers. On the other hand rights offerings may have undesirable consequences such as causing a decrease in the price of the firm's stock and requiring adverse changes in the terms of the firm's convertible securities. Several explanations have been proposed about why some firms choose rights offerings and others do not. We consider some of these explanations:

---

[1] See Logue, Dennis E. and James K. Seward (1992).
[2] Bohren, Øyvind, B. Espen Eckbo, and Dag Michalsen, 1997.

Table 1-3. Trading prices (in EUR) and volume for UniCredit

Date	Open†	Close†	Volume
Jan 31, 2012	3.65	3.79	172,163,100
Jan 30, 2012	3.58	3.56	155,372,000
Jan 27, 2012	3.78	3.65	140,653,500
Jan 26, 2012	3.88	3.82	150,243,100
Jan 25, 2012	3.80	3.80	188,481,100
Jan 24, 2012	3.66	3.75	132,550,900
Jan 23, 2012	3.39	3.66	175,607,800
Jan 20, 2012	3.27	3.31	220,424,800
Jan 19, 2012	3.03	3.36	278,713,600
Jan 18, 2012	3.00	2.98	115,866,900
Jan 17, 2012	3.01	3.01	164,767,300
Jan 16, 2012	2.78	2.93	133,534,200
Jan 13, 2012	2.98	2.92	194,758,400
Jan 12, 2012	2.61	2.90	270,820,700
Jan 11, 2012	2.43	2.56	160,073,300
Jan 10, 2012	2.32	2.42	230,025,700
Jan 9, 2012	2.67	2.29	173,439,300
Jan 6, 2012	4.37	3.98	115,194,500
Jan 5, 2012	5.25	4.48	61,691,200
Jan 4, 2012	6.28	5.41	43,640,300
Nov 3, 2012	7.58	8.32	20,494,200

Source: Yahoo finance.

1. Convertible wealth transfer hypothesis

If a firm's outstanding convertible securities contain an anti-dilution clause, then issuing rights at a discount can trigger an automatic reduction in conversion rates.¹ A convertible security is one that, under certain conditions, can convert from debt to equity or from equity to debt. The value of the bonds is increased without any compensation for the firm, shifting wealth from equity holders. Thus, firms with convertible securities have an added incentive to avoid issuing rights with deep discounts.

2. Information asymmetry

At least two models have been developed that explain the choice of rights versus underwritten offering based on information asymmetries. The first emphasizes that the underwriter may provide certification that the issue is a worthwhile investment.² This certification is necessary because corporate insiders who know more about the prospects of the firm than outsiders might only sell stock that is overpriced. Recognizing this, investors an underwriter may be necessary to allay investors' fears.

In the U.S., the certification services provided by an investment banker consist chiefly of meeting the due diligence requirement of section 11 **of** the Securities and Exchange Act of 1933. Included in this requirement is the expert certification of financial and legal information contained in the registration statement. Moreover, work by Beatty and Ritter (1986), Johnson and Miller (1988), and Carter and Manaster (1990) suggests that underwriter involvement in an equity issue can reduce the information asymmetry between the firm and investors. They further note that lower-quality firms tend to avoid the scrutiny of a public underwriter by using rights financing.

A second model based on information asymmetries emphasizes differences in firm quality.³ In this model lower-quality firms use a public offering and employ an uninformed underwriter. Higher-quality firms use rights offerings. Within the set of firms using rights offerings, the highest-quality firms signal their high quality by employing a standby underwriter; the remaining firms signal their quality by choosing an appropriate

---

[1] See Eckbo and Masulis (1992).
[2] Booth and Smith (1986) extend the work of Klein and Leffler (1981) on reputational signaling to develop this model.
[3] See Heinkel and Schwartz (1986).

subscription price: the higher the price, the higher the quality of the firm.[1]

3. Transactions costs hypothesis

The transaction costs hypothesis contends that the choice of offer type depends on the relative cost of underwritten and rights offerings.[2] The price of existing shares falls significantly before the offering date of a rights offering,[3] but underwritten issues are not associated with any abnormal offering-period price behavior.[4] The price decline before a rights offering is viewed as compensation for transactions costs incurred by the buyers, including portfolio adjustment costs, commissions, taxes, and the like. If investors are to be induced to exercise rights rather than purchase shares outright, they must be compensated for any extra cost and effort involved. Hence the price of the firm's stock is expected to decline before the rights offering and then rebound, with the rebound providing the compensation.

An alternate view of the transactions cost hypothesis is presented by another study that finds that bid-ask spreads increase following rights offerings, but decline following public offerings.[5] These findings are attributed to the fact that rights offerings lead to more concentrated ownership and public offerings lead to more dispersed ownership. Hence,

---

[1] Bhagat (1983) presents the delay in the acquisition of equity funds and the uncertainty of offering success as costs associated with a rights issue. Heinkel and Schwartz recognize a distinction between an insured (standby) and an uninsured rights offering and introduce a standby agreement fee which serves as an additional cost. Heinkel and Schwartz also argue that the highest-quality firms incorporate a standby agreement in their rights offers that involves an exogenous fixed investigative cost to the underwriter. Intermediate-quality firms, however, simply use an uninsured rights offer.

[2] This hypothesis was originally developed by Kraus and Stoll (1972) and later examined by Hansen and Pinkerton (1982) and Hansen (1988).

[3] See Hansen (1988).

[4] Included among the studies that report no significant excess returns for underwritten offerings during either the pre- or post-offering period are Smith (1977), and Mikkelson and Partch (1986).

[5] Kothare (1997).

companies with actively traded shares would tend to prefer underwritten offerings.

4. Agency cost argument

Another explanation of the choice between rights and underwritten offers involves agency conflicts that can be present in the modern corporation.[1] The first is the possibility that managers and board members may receive benefits from the use of underwriters that do not accrue to the firm's general shareholders. The firm's board of directors may include an investment banker,[2] or the investment banking firm may allocate oversubscribed issues to the managers. Choice of issuing method also has implications for the monitoring of the firm's activities. The greater dispersion in share ownership resulting from a public offering may reduce the ability of shareholders to monitor the firm.

5. Local institutional considerations

Sometimes a firm may be constrained in setting the subscription price for a rights offering based on the par value of the stock. The par value of a stock is the value stated in the corporate charter. In Japan it has been customary to set the offering price at the par value of the firm. This practice works if the stock price is just above the par value. Then the exercise price will be below the market price and the rights will be exercised. But if the stock price is below the par value a rights offering would not be possible, because the stock can be purchased more cheaply in the market than it can be obtained by exercising the rights. Also, if the price of the stock is substantially greater than the par value a firm might be discouraged from using a rights offering. In Japan firms frequently base their dividends on par value. Therefore, an increase in outstanding shares leads to an increase in dividends. Suppose that a stock's par value were 10 JPY and its market price is 90 JPY. To raise 90 JPY requires the sale of one new share using a secondary offering and the sale of nine new shares using a rights offering.

---

[1] See Smith (1977).

[2] Herman (1981) reports that 21% of the 200 largest non-financial and 27% of the 100 largest industrial firms include at least one investment banker on their board of directors.

In the second case the firm's dividend is increased by nine times as much as in the first case. Therefore, a firm with a high stock price compared with par value might prefer a secondary offering.

3. Equity investment vehicles

3.1. Pooled investment plans

Plans, called by various names such as pooled investment plans or collective investment schemes, in which the funds of many individuals are combined and invested jointly are a very popular way for individuals to buy securities. These plans are available to investors in most countries. In the U.S. there are actually more pooled investment plans than there are operating firms trading on the New York Stock Exchange.

There are many differences throughout the world in the way investment funds are organized and operated. The corporate form of organization is predominant in the U.S., but the trust form is predominant elsewhere.

3.1.1. Pooled investment plans in the U.S.

In the U.S. collective investment schemes are regulated under the Investment Company Act of 1940. As defined under the 1940 Act, investment companies include any issuer that is engaged primarily in the business of investing or trading in securities or that holds securities with a value exceeding 40% of the issuer's assets. The 1940 Act itself, or regulations issued by the USSEC, exempt a variety of companies including investment bankers and securities brokers, financial institutions, trust funds managed by banks, and companies engaged in operations through subsidiaries from the 1940 Acts provisions. There are two main types of regulated investment companies—unit investment trusts and managed investment companies.

Unit investment trusts (UIT) own a fixed pool of securities in which each investor has an interest proportionate to their contribution. (Note that UITs should not be confused with unit trusts described below.) The UIT is organized under a trust indenture or similar arrangement, does not have a board of directors, and issues only redeemable securities representing an undivided interest in the UIT's portfolio. The UIT is designed for investors who seek diversification, but do not want active management. UITs most commonly hold fixed-income securities issued by the various states and their subdivisions (counties, cities, airport, sewer, school authorities, and the like). These fixed-income securities are known collectively as municipal bonds.

Managed investment companies are organized as corporations with a board of directors. Investors purchase shares in the corporation that represent an undivided interest in the firm's assets. Net asset value is the value of the assets owned by an investment company less its liabilities. Net asset value is often stated on a per share basis. There are two main types of managed investment companies—closed-end and open-end.

Closed-end investment companies have a fixed number of outstanding shares and only rarely raise new funds. Because they thought the name closed-end was confusing, these types of investment companies have switched to calling themselves publicly-traded investment companies. Closed-end fund shares are traded in the secondary markets just like the shares of operating companies. Investors purchasing or selling these shares pay brokerage commissions and incur other costs just like those paid when trading other securities. There are many closed-end investment company shares traded on NASDAQ and listed on the NYSE. Since the value of closed-end fund shares is determined by supply and demand, the market price can be more or less than net asset value.

Open-end investment companies, which are also called mutual funds, are continually issuing new shares. Because they are issuing new shares in the U.S. they must have a registration statement in effect. There is little or no secondary market trading so the shares are not traded on exchanges. The purchase and sale price (not including fees) is net asset value. Investors buy their shares directly from the fund through a distributor. Many distributors charge a load or commission at the time of the purchase. For stock funds this load was often as high as 8-9% of the purchase price, but with increased competition loads of 4-5% are more common today.[1] While the

---

[1] The two largest mutual fund groups in the US are Fidelity Investments and Vanguard Group. You can obtain more information at web sites whose addresses are, respectively:
http://www441.fidelity.com:80/, and http://www.vanguard.com/.

load is typically charged at the time of the purchase, for a rear-end load, the fee is charged when the shares are redeemed. In the late 1940s investors in the U.S. were unfamiliar with mutual funds so most funds hired sales forces that received a part of the load as compensation. Even today many mutual funds are distributed through brokerage firms or distributors who charge a load. But as investors have increasingly become familiar with mutual funds, there has been substantial growth in no load mutual funds, funds that do not charge a commission. True no-load funds do not have either a front- or rear-end load. Table 1-4 provides information about the portfolios and expenses of a few mutual funds.

3.1.2. Pooled investment plans outside the U.S.

The principal type of collective investment scheme in many countries is the contractual-type that is often referred to as unit trusts. A unit trust is an agreement, evidenced by a trust deed, between a trustee and an investment manager under which the investment manager will purchase securities (or sometimes other assets such as real estate or precious metals). The manager divides the beneficial interest in these assets into units for sale to investors. Each investor owns an interest in direct proportion to the unit trusts contributed. The unit trusts are invested by the fund manager acting for the investors.

Countries with significant assets invested in unit trusts include Australia, Hong Kong, and Korea. In Japan all collective investment schemes are contractual-type and unit trusts also are well established in countries such as the United Kingdom and Singapore.[1]

Some closed-type unit trusts permit redemptions during the life of the fund and other have no distributions before the termination of the trust. Stock unit trusts that invest in domestic and non-Japanese issues and index funds are typically of the open-type. There are both unit-type and open-type unit trusts that invest in stocks and bonds for income. Stock investment

---

[1] In the US the Investment Company Institute provides a large amount of information about mutual funds in the US, including statistics that show that the asset holdings of these funds total about 5,000 billion USD. The Institute's web address is: http://www.ici.org/.

Table 1-4. Portfolio composition and costs of selected mutual funds

Cash	Stock US	Stock Non-US	Bond	Other
Panel A: Portfolio composition				
Fidelity Large Cap Core Enhanced Index FLCEX				
2.01%	95.74%	2.24%	0.00%	0.00%
Fidelity Small Cap Enhanced Index FCPEX				
3.85%	95.57%	0.59%	0.00%	0.00%
Fidelity Advisor Global Bond A FGBZX				
38.80%	0.00%	0.00%	56.21%	4.99%

Initial	Deferred	Redemption
Panel B: Maximum sales fees		
Fidelity Small Cap Enhanced Index FCPEX		
na	na	1.50% < 90 days; 0 > 90 days
Fidelity Large Cap Core Enhanced Index FLCEX		
na	na	na
Fidelity Advisor Global Bond A FGBZX		
4.00%	na	na

NER	Management	12-b1	Admin.	Waivers
Panel C: Other fees/expenses				
Fidelity Small Cap Enhanced Index FCPEX				
0.67%	0.52%	na	na	na
Fidelity Large Cap Core Enhanced Index FLCEX				
0.45%	0.35%	-	na	na
Fidelity Advisor Global Bond A FGBZX				
1.00%	0.57%	0.25%	na	na

Notes: na = not applicable Panel B: Initial sales fees (front-end loads) are paid when the fund is purchased and typically go to a broker. Deferred sales fees are paid when the fund is sold and also typically go to a broker. Redemption fees typically go to the fund to offset transactions costs. Panel C: NER = net expense ratio; 12-b1 fees are paid by the fund, reducing performance, and are for marketing expenses incurred by the fund; Funds sometimes waive (Waivers) expenses to make a fund look more competitive and encourage sales. Expenses are actual expenses.

Source: Morningstar
http://quicktake.morningstar.com/fundfamily/fidelity-investments/0C00001YR0/fund-list.aspx (February 2013)

trusts can invest in both stocks and bonds, but bond investment trusts invest exclusively in fixed income securities.

Unit trusts available outside the U.S. typically charge a load. The US GROWTH FUND offered by DBS Asset Management Ltd. of Singapore is typical. The offer price includes a sales commission of 5% with discounts available for one-time purchases exceeding 100,000 SGD. Five Arrows Asian Enterprise Trust's (Five Arrows) prospectus provides for a Realization Charge of up to 2% at the time of the sale or the redemption of the units. According to the prospectus, the fee "shall be retained by the managers for their own benefit." This fee is similar to rear-end load. Dividends may be automatically reinvested in units of the trust, but unlike the practice in the U.S. where this reinvestment is usually at net asset value, many non-U.S. unit trusts charge a load for reinvested dividends.[1]

The Undertakings for Collective Investment in Transferable Securities (UCITS) provides regulations under which mutual unit trusts registered in one EU country can be sold in all the other EU member states. The regulations provide for diversification of assets and limits on holdings of particular types of assets.[2]

---

[1] The Investment Management Association (IMA) was formed in the UK in 1959 to act as a representative body for its members. It has over 116 unit trust and investment fund managers as Members, with nearly £100 billion funds under management, and represents over 79% of the unit trust industry in the UK. Its web address is: http://preview.iii.co.uk/autif/. The IMA provides a glossary at: http://preview.iii.co.uk/autif/gloss/. A site that provides free, daily comparative performance data and detailed information covering 600 UK investment trusts and closed ended offshore funds is: http://www.trustnet.co.uk/. Web addresses of sites in other countries include: Hong Kong Standard Tigernet http://www.hkstandard.com/online/finance/007/mfunds/main.htm; Association of Unit Trusts and Investment Funds (UK), http://www.iii.co.uk/autif/about/; Investment Trust Association (Japan) http://www.highway.or.jp/toushin/index.htm.

[2] http://www.lavenpartners.com/wp-content/uploads/2011/05/Laven-Definitive-Guidebook-to-UCITS-IV-Funds.pdf

In Japan, the unit trusts can be either open-type in that new unit trusts are accepted for investment during the life of the fund or closed-type for which no new unit trusts are accepted. Open-type unit trusts typically allow redemptions at a price that represents a pro rata share of net asset value. equities, derivatives, and other mutual funds), and monitoring of risk. Ineligible assets are real estate and direct holdings (as opposed as through derivatives) of commodities and metals.[1]

3.1.3. Fees of pooled investment plans

In addition to loads, which are paid directly by investors, there are typically other fees that are charged against the assets of pooled investments so that investors pay these charges indirectly. Management fees are the most important and common indirect expense. DBS Asset Management charges an annual fee of 1.25% of net asset value of its US GROWTH FUND while Rothschild Asset Management charges 1.5% annually for managing Five Arrows. The trustee's fee for Five Arrows can be as much as 0.25% of net asset value annually. These fee levels are higher than the 0.5% to 1.0% typically in the U.S. Naturally, pooled investment funds pay the costs of operating the fund including taxes, brokerage commissions, legal and accounting fees, and the like. In some jurisdictions such as Singapore and the U.S. advertising costs associated with selling the fund can be charged to the fund. In the U.S. section 12b-1 of the 1940 Act permits the payment of an extra fee to the fund's management company out of fund assets to help defray marketing costs. In the U.S. more than 60% of all mutual funds assess a **12b-1 fee**. These fees typically range from 0.25% to 1% of net asset value.

In the U.S. a few funds charge a transactions fee payable directly to the fund at the time of the purchase or sale of the fund. These fees are distinguished from loads, which are payments to the manager and distributor. These transactions fees are designed to help defray the costs of establishing and eliminating positions due to shareholder turnover. Transactions charges of this type are most common for funds investing in

---

[1] https://www2.blackrock.com/webcore/litService/search/getDocument.seam?venue=PUB_IND&source=GLOBAL&contentId=1111125006

securities that are difficult or costly to purchase and sell such as those in emerging markets.

3.2. Index funds

There are several exchange-traded pooled investment funds. In May 1987, the Toronto Stock Exchange created a trust that holds baskets of the stocks in the Toronto 35 index for investors wishing to own a diversified portfolio of senior Canadian corporations. Units representing an interest in the trust are traded on the Toronto Stock Exchange. Investors holding a prescribed number of units can redeem them for the underlying basket of stocks and investors owning the underlying basket can submit them to the trust in exchange for units of the trust. The designated market maker on the floor of the exchange actively arbitrages the units and the underlying baskets.

In January 1993 the American Stock Exchange began trading shares of an **exchange-traded fund (ETFs)**. These shares are a beneficial interest (Standard and Poor Depository Receipts, abbreviated SPDRs and pronounced "spiders") in a unit investment trust that holds a portfolio of all common stocks in the Standard and Poor's 500 Index. The fund had one of the fastest fund launches in U.S. history growing to 700 million USD by mid 1995. Investors can deposit shares comprising the underlying portfolio with a custodial bank and receive shares of beneficial interest in return. These shares of beneficial interest are then traded like other stocks listed on exchanges. The shares of beneficial interest can also be submit to the custodial bank and redeemed for the underlying shares. This ability to create and destroy the shares of beneficial interest enables arbitrageurs to keep the trading prices in line with the fund's asset value.

In 1996 trading began on the American Stock Exchange in another open-end fund, World Equity Benchmark Shares Foreign Fund, Inc. Units of the fund are called "WEBS" in a word play on the earlier spiders. The fund is managed as seventeen separate portfolios, called series, each designed to match the performance of the market in a particular country, namely: Australia, Austria, Belgium, Canada, France, Germany, Hong Kong, Italy, Japan, Malaysia, Mexico, The Netherlands, Singapore, Spain, Sweden, Switzerland, and the United Kingdom. BZW Barclays Global Fund Advisors is responsible for the investment management of each series and this management will include the use of portfolio optimization techniques. In 1996 six Singapore banks created an open-end mutual fund to invest in companies included in the Straits Times Regional Market Index. The DIAMONDS Trust, which began trading on the American Stock Exchange on Jan. 20, 1998, is a unit investment trust designed to track the performance of the Dow Jones Industrial Average through its holdings of the stocks in that index.[1]

In addition to being exchange traded, ETFs often have very low fees because of their fixed portfolios. In recent years there has been a proliferation of ETFs so that in addition to having ETFs holding well diversified portfolios there are many ETFs that hold portfolios of particular industries. There are also ETFs that hold commodities such as gold and oil.[2]

3.3. Hedge funds

A **hedge fund** is an investment organization whose management receives compensation in the form of performance incentives rather than or in addition to fees based on the amount of assets held or the number of transactions made.[3] Typically, the managers are also substantial investors in the fund. In the U.S. hedge funds are structured as corporations or partnerships. By raising funds through a private placement the hedge fund avoids registration under the Investment Company Act of 1940, which imposes substantial limitations on the types of investments that can be made. These U.S. hedge funds cannot make a general solicitation. Funds can be raised in private offerings to an unlimited number of accredited investors, but non-accredited investors are limited to 35. An **accredited investor** is an established financial institution such as a bank, brokerage firm or insurance company, certain pension plans and wealthy individuals. To avoid registration the hedge fund is limited to no more than 100

---

[1] Information on SPDRs, WEBS, and DIAMONDS can be obtained from the American Stock Exchange web address: http://www.amex.com/.
[2] http://en.wikipedia.org/wiki/Exchange-traded_fund
[3] For information on Van Hedge Fund Advisors International, which tracks hedge funds see: http://www.vanhedge.com/indexes.html.

beneficial owners. Naturally, hedge fund managers seek to raise as much as they can from this limited group so that in practice minimum investments in U.S.-based hedge funds are typically 250,000 USD or more.

Hedge funds are also organized outside the U.S. Depending on the laws of the particular jurisdiction, these funds can be organized either as partnerships or corporations. As long as the investors in the fund come from outside the local jurisdiction, limitations on the raising of funds are not typically imposed. In the U.S. these hedge funds are referred to as offshore and they are not open to U.S. investors. Popular jurisdictions for hedge funds include Bermuda, the Cayman Islands, Curacao, the British Virgin Islands, the Bahamas, Luxembourg, Dublin (Ireland), Gibraltar, Liechtenstein, Switzerland, and Mauritius. Several European Community countries require registration, which has spurred the growth of Dublin as an offshore center and a number of offshore funds are listed on the Dublin Stock Exchange.

The first hedge fund is attributed to Alfred Winslow Jones, who was born in Australia and moved to the U.S. with his family at the age of four. Jones established an investment partnership and measured market exposure using the following formula:

$$\text{Market exposure} = (\text{Long exposure} - \text{Short exposure}) / \text{Capital}$$

Jones's idea was to judiciously select equities that were expected to outperform the market and to finance the purchases of these equities by selling short the equities of securities there were not expected to outperform the market. This strategy places total emphasis on the manager's stock selection capability. Since historically equities have yielded positive returns, Jones did not seek to have zero market exposure. Jones's investment results were impressive, outperforming all mutual funds over a ten-year period. An article published in 1966 in the U.S. magazine Fortune lead to a spate of new hedge funds. In 1968, the USSEC found 140 partnerships functioning as hedge funds, most having been formed in that year.

Today hedge funds follow a variety of investment strategies. The most common are:

Market neutral—this is an extreme version of the Jones approach in which the manager seeks very low or zero market exposure.

Event-driven—the manager seeks arbitrage opportunities in bankruptcy securities and mergers.

Opportunistic—the manager takes advantage of opportunities wherever they are found so that exposure to various markets and strategies changes. Global funds pay attention to economic developments around the world seeking investment opportunities. Some specialize in particular types of markets (e.g., emerging markets) or particular regions.

Derivatives—managers use all types of derivatives including those covering foreign exchange.

Most hedge funds use derivatives extensively both because of the leverage they provide and because they can allow exposure to markets where cash instruments are either nonexistent or illiquid.

An example of an opportunity that attracted hedge funds with varied investment strategies arose in 1997. A number of closed-end investment companies in Taiwan were selling at discounts of about twenty percent from net asset value. Under Taiwanese law the shareholders of a fund that sells at a discount of more than 20% for more than 20 consecutive days can call a special shareholders meeting and liquidate the fund. Seeing an opportunity, a number of hedge funds began buying the closed-end funds and offsetting the risk of these investments using derivatives.

4. Problems faced by international investors

This section describes two types of risk faced by international investors: (1) unfavorable political, economic, financial risk in their home county, and (2) foreign share ownership restrictions. We discuss currencies, which are also a source of risk, are discussed in Chapter 4.

4.1. Country risk

International investors face country risks arising from the political and economic conditions in a particular country. Inflation, exchange controls, and tax regulations differ across countries.[1] Governments frequently change regulations to the disadvantage of non-domestic investors. In 1997,

---

[1] Country Risk Monitor ranks 80 countries for current and future business risk on the basis of the following criteria: (1) Ability to pay foreign debt., (2)

following a major drop in the value of Malaysian equities, the Malaysian government announced a series of measures including the purchase of equities from domestic investors at above market prices and restrictions on the transfer of securities. Although these regulations and policies were either short-lived of never implemented, they indicate the potential for such measures. Institutional Investor, a U.S. magazine, publishes a country risk index for 112 countries every six months. The index is constructed from the results of a survey of 75-100 banks located outside the country being assessed. Political Risk Services publishes an International Country Risk Guide covering 130 countries. Political risks include thirteen factors such as racial and national tensions, military in politics, external conflict risk, and corruption in government. Financial risk factors include factors such as expropriation by government, repudiation of contracts by the government, and losses due to exchange controls. Economic risks include factors such as inflation and strength of the currency. International portfolios contain significant country risk.[1] In fact, according to Madura, Tucker, and Wiley (1997), "the most relevant factor explaining disparate returns across markets is country risk." Equity returns are higher for high credit risk countries and volatility of returns is about the same as that for low credit risk countries.[2]

Strength of trade performance, (3) Government fiscal responsibility, (4) Foreign indebtedness, (5) Income per capita, (6) Involvement in international trade. Their web address is:
http://www.bofa.com/econ_indicator/monitor.html. CMS's International Country Risk Guide covers 130 countries with country-by-country information on the comparative risk of lending or operating in each country. Their web address is: http://www.textor.com/cms/dPRIC.html.
[1] Ranjan, Murli, and Jodeph Freidman (1997).
[2] See Erb, Harvey and Viskanta (1995).For a web site that deals with country risk and provides a comparison of various country risk services see: http://stocks.miningco.com/library/weekly/aa081897.htm.

4.2. Foreign ownership restrictions

In many countries, the percentage of common stock that can be held by foreign investors is limited. As shown in Box 1-1 and Box 1-2 these restrictions can potentially result in serious problems for international investors. Usually the foreign and domestic shares provide identical claims on the cash flows of the company. Limitations on foreign ownership may come about either through governmental laws and regulations or through restrictions in a company's corporate charter or by-laws. The German Foreign Trade Act restricts foreign ownership of defense firms and airlines. Italy restricts ownership in banking, shipping and airlines. U.S. restrictions on the percentage of foreign ownership allowed for U.S. commercial television stations led Australian Rupert Murdoch to become a U.S. citizen.

Countries also differ in the way these restrictions are administered. Before 1986 Finland restricted the percentage of Finish companies that could be owned by non-citizens and prohibited citizens from owning equities of non-Finnish companies. Eighty percent of the shares carried a stamp showing that their ownership was restricted to Finnish citizens. Thus, Finnish investors could buy either restricted or unrestricted shares, but non-Finnish investors could only purchase the restricted shares. Before 1983 foreign investors had little interest in Finnish shares. But then demand grew to the point that brokers had difficulty finding unrestricted shares to satisfy the foreign demand. There was only one price quotation on the exchange, but sellers were willing to sell only restricted shares at this price. Brokers were forced to form an unofficial market in unrestricted shares until 1984 when the exchange began to quote restricted and unrestricted shares separately.

Singapore had a system much like that in Finland. Foreign investors typically can buy shares from a domestic investor and register them as foreign-owned as long as the ownership restriction level has not been reached. Once the restriction has been reached, foreign investors can only be assured of being able to register their shares if they purchase them from another foreign investor. Singaporeans are allowed to purchase foreign registered shares and retain the foreign registration. Once the foreign ownership restriction becomes binding, foreign- and domestically-registered shares are quoted separately.

> **Box 1-1. Bank Bali's international shareholders burned by local investors seeking a quick profit**
>
> In June 1995 Bank Bali, Indonesia's seventh largest commercial bank in terms of assets, had a rights offering that left international shareholders with substantial losses.
>
> Indonesian laws limit foreign ownership in a listed company to 49 per cent. And the foreign ownership percentage was at its limit prior to the rights offering. The offering of 65.134 million new shares was fully subscribed.
>
> A loophole in Indonesia's regulations allows local shareholders to register new shares from a rights issue under the foreign category on a first-come-first-served-basis. Local shareholders rushed to register their shares in the foreign category. Their motive was to benefit from the 36% premium accorded foreign-registered shares.
>
> Foreign investors owning about 4 million shares were able to exercise their rights, but owners of about 27 million shares were not. "A whole lot of guys out there feel cheated," said a senior analyst who follows the bank.
>
> A senior director of Bank Bali indicated that what happened was legal and the rule that the local investors followed was highlighted in the prospects. Moreover, registering local shares as foreign was said to be common practice. However, in cases in which the foreign ownership restriction is already binding, this loophole harms foreign inventors.
>
> Source: Leslie Lopez, Asian Wall Street Journal, July 1995.

Usually the shares owned by domestic investors and those owned by foreign investors have equal claims to assets and dividends and to vote. If the percentage of foreign ownership is below permitted levels, then the restrictions on foreign ownership have no practical effect. But when the restriction becomes binding, difficulties may arise. A binding restriction says, in effect, that the supply of foreign-registered stock is not sufficient to satisfy the demand of foreign investors who have a higher assessment of the value of the firm than local investors. The foreign-registered shares become more valuable since these shares also carry the foreign registration.

> **Box 1-2. Qantas**
>
> In July 1995, the Australian government used an initial public offering to sell shares in Qantas Airways worth more than 1 billion USD and representing a 75% ownership stake. British Airways owns the remaining 25%. The government stipulated that Qantas's foreign ownership cannot exceed 49% and further that no foreign airline can own more that 35%.
>
> On the first day of trading more than 73 million shares changed hands and Qantas said that it had no way of knowing the nationality of buyers because the company was still mailing shares to shareholders. The shares are currently trading on a deferred-settlement basis and the company will not be able to assess the level of foreign ownership for several weeks.
>
> Qantas said that under its articles of association and the Qantas Sale Act, the Qantas board is obliged to ensure that the maximum aggregate foreign-share-ownership limits are enforced. After three weeks, Qantas announced that foreign investors had purchased 52% of its shares and that these investors would be required to sell 3.1 million shares during the next 90 days on a last in first out basis.
>
> Sources: Asian Wall Street Journal, August 2, 1995, p.18 and August 12, 1995, p. 11.

Evidence has been offered supporting several explanations for differences in prices between foreign and domestic shares. One possibility is that foreign investors seek to create capitalization-weighted portfolios of shares for a particular country. If the desired investment level exceeded the foreign shares available, these shares would sell at a premium to the local shares, and the premium would be greater for firms with more stringent foreign ownership restrictions. Consistent with this view, the premiums of foreign shares over domestic shares are greater for firms with tighter foreign ownership restrictions. Another reason that foreign shares are more valuable is that they are typically more liquid. Foreign investors, being less familiar with local firms, typically need more information to make their investment decisions. Also, firms with greater availability of information have a larger premium.[1]

Historically, China allowed the issuance of three types of shares. A shares are listed on the Shanghai or Shenzhen stock exchanges and are traded in local currency. B shares are traded on the same exchanges, but initially were open only to foreign ownership. Later domestic Chinese were also permitted to own these shares. B shares are traded in HKD in Shenzhen and in USD in Shanghai. Companies that can meet higher standards can issue H shares that are listed in Hong Kong and traded in HKD. These shares can be owned by anyone except domestic Chinese. Some companies that are not incorporated in China, but have their primary business in China, are traded on the London Stock Exchange (and sometime called L shares) or in the U.S. (and called N shares).[2] Companies that are incorporated in China can also have ADRs of their H shares listed in New York.

5. Summary

In this chapter we describe the characteristics of equity securities including common stock, preferred stock, and warrants. We also provide additional details about rights offerings not covered in earlier chapters. We describe the creation of depository receipts that allow the trading on non-U.S. stocks in the U.S. Sometimes common stock is divided into classes, each with different rights, especially in voting. Preferred stock has a claim that is superior to that of common stock but inferior to that of the firm's debtors.[3] Usually firms can use preferred stock equity to meet any capital requirements imposed by regulators. Most preferred stock has a cumulative provision requiring that preferred stock obligations be met before any common stock dividends can be paid. There are a number of different types of preferred stock. Convertible preferred stock can be exchanged for

---

[1] See Bailey and Jagtiani (1994).

[2] http://mobius.blog.franklintempleton.com/2012/10/16/the-abcs-of-chinas-share-markets/

[3] Superior claims are paid prior to inferior claims.

another security, typically common stock in the issuer. Floating rate preferred stock has a dividend rate that is reset periodically.

In 1927, the U.S. investment banking firm, J.P. Morgan, created the American Depository Receipt (ADR) to simplify investment in non-U.S. companies by U.S. investors. Many countries throughout the world now have their own version of DRs. In the U.S. there are over 900 DR programs with issuers from more than 40 countries and DRs are traded on the New York and American Stock Exchanges, on NASDAQ, and over-the-counter. DRs are easier to trade because they are traded in the local market, usually in local currency, and the depository arranges for the conversion of dividends into local currency.

A warrant is a security giving the owner a claim to an underlying interest at a specified price before a specified time. Warrants are both equities and derivatives. Warrants are used by firms to raise equity capital both at the time of issue, and, if the warrant is exercised, at a later time. Warrants have also been used in acquisitions. It is becoming more common for financial institutions to create covered warrants by purchasing underlying interests and then issuing warrants.

Rights offerings are used to raise equity capital. While the use of rights has declined in the U.S., they are still used extensively in many countries including Japan and the U.K. Many explanations have been proposed about why some firms choose rights offerings and others do not. Anti-dilution clauses in convertible indentures may argue against the use of rights offering. Firms may employ underwriters to allay investors fears that firms only issue stock when it is overpriced. Rights offerings may have hidden costs in that price declines in the firm's stock value offset underwriting savings. Managers may choose underwritten offerings because they receive benefits from the underwriters.

Pooled investment plans are a common way for individuals and small institutions to invest. These plans are available to investors in most countries. In the U.S. there are more pooled investment plans than there are operating firms trading on the New York Stock Exchange. Unit investment trusts own a fixed pool of securities. In contrast, both open-end and closed-end investment companies manage their portfolios. Closed-end investment companies have a fixed number of shares outstanding whereas open-end investment companies are continuously issuing new shares. The distributors of some closed-end investment companies (also called mutual funds) charge a commission or load when the shares are initially purchased, but no load mutual funds can be bought without a commission.

Outside the U.S. unit trusts are the most common type of pooled investment scheme. A unit trust is an agreement, evidenced by a trust deed, between a trustee and an investment manager under which the investment manager will purchase securities. The manager divides the beneficial interest in these assets into units for sale to investors. Each investor owns an interest in direct proportion to the funds contributed. The funds are invested by the fund manager acting for investors in a portfolio of marketable securities.

In many countries there are limits on the percentage of equity that non-domestic investors can hold. These restrictions often vary from industry to industry. When the percentage of shares owned by foreigners reaches its limit, it is common to trade the foreign-registered and domestically-registered separately.

Questions

1. How have computers improved clearing and settlement?
2. Why is knowledge of clearing and settlement methods and institutions more important for those investing internationally?
3. Besides the increasing use of computers, name two other changes in practices that have improved clearing and settlement.
4. What are the obstacles to achieving perfect delivery versus payment?
5. What problems might arise if an earthquake destroyed a central depository's computer?
6. How do covered warrants differ from traditional warrants?
7. What are two possible explanations that might explain why a firm would choose an underwritten offer rather than a rights offering?
8. Explain why rights offerings do not increase the value of the firm.
9. What is the difference between a load and no-load mutual fund
10. How can restrictions on foreign ownership result in equities that have a claim on the same cash flows having different values?
11. What is the difference between a unit investment trust and a unit trust?

12. What are the advantages of depository receipts over owning the underlying security? Are there disadvantages?

References

Akerlof, George A., 1970, The market for "lemons": Quality and the market mechanism, Quarterly Journal of Economics 84, 488-500.

Bailey, Warren, and Julapa Jagtiani, 1994, Foreign ownership restrictions and stock prices in the Thai capital market, Journal of Financial Economics 36, 57-87.

Balachandran, Balasingham, Robert Faff, and Michael Theobald, 2008, Rights offerings, takeup, renounceability, and underwriting status, Journal of Financial Economics 89, 328-346.

Beatty Randolph P., and Jay R. Ritter, 1986, Investment banking, reputation and the underpricing of initial public offerings, Journal of Financial Economics 15, 213-232.

Bhagat, Sanjai, 1983, The effect of preemptive right amendments on shareholder wealth, Journal of Financial Economics 12, 287-310.

Booth, James R., and Richard L. Smith, 1986, Capital raising, underwriting and the certification hypothesis, Journal of Financial Economics 15, 261-281.

Carter, Richard B., and Steve Manaster, 1990, Initial public offerings and underwriter reputation, Journal of Finance 45, 1045-1067.

Cronqvist, Henrik, 2005, The choice between rights offerings and private equity placements, Journal of Financial Economics 78, 375–407.

Eckbo, B. Espen, and Ronald W. Masulis, 1992, Adverse selection and the rights offer paradox, Journal of Financial Economics 32, 293-332.

Eckbo, B. Espen, and Savita Verma, 1994, Managerial share ownership, voting power and cash dividend policy, Journal of Corporate Finance 1, 33-62.

Eun, Cheol S., and S. Janakiramanan, 1986, A model of international asset pricing with a constraint on the foreign equity ownership, Journal of Finance 41, 897-914.

Ferris, Andrew F., 1991, The Financial Markets of Hong Kong. London: Routledge.

Ferris, Stephen P., Gregory Noronha, and Thomas H. McInish, 1997, New equity offerings in Japan: an examination of theory and practice, Journal of International Financial Markets, Institutions and Money 7, 185-200.

Hansen, Robert S., 1988, The demise of the rights issue, Review of Financial Studies 1, 289-309.

Hansen, Robert S., and John M. Pinkerton, 1982, Direct equity financing: a resolution of a paradox, Journal of Finance 37, 651-665.

Heinkel, Robert, and Eduardo S. Schwartz, 1986, Rights versus underwritten offerings: an asymmetric information approach, Journal of Finance 41, 1-18.

Hietala, Pekka T., 1989, Asset pricing in partially segmented markets: Evidence from the Finnish market, Journal of Finance 44, 697-718.

Herman, Edward S., 1981, Corporate Control, Corporate Power. Cambridge University Press: New York, NY.

Holderness, Clifford G., Randall S. Kroszner, and Dennis P. Sheehan. 1999, "Were the Good Old Days That Good? Changes in Managerial Stock Ownership since the Great Depression." Journal of Finance 54, 435-69.

Johnson, James M., and Robert .E. Miller, 1988, Investment banker prestige and the underpricing of initial public offerings, Financial Management 17, 19-29.

Klein, Benjamin, and Keith Leffler, 1981, The role of market forces in assuring contractual performance, Journal of Political Economy 89, 615-641.

Kothare, M., 1997, The Effects of equity issues on ownership structure and stock liquidity: A comparison of rights and public offerings, Journal of Financial Economics 43, 131-148.

Kraus, Allen, and Hans R. Stoll, 1972, Price impacts of block trading on the New York Stock Exchange, Journal of Finance 27, 569-588.

Loderer, Claudio, and Heinz Zimmerman, 1988, Stock offerings in a different institutional setting: the Swiss case, 1973-1983, Journal of Banking and Finance 12, 353-378.

López de Silanes, Florencio, Rafael La Porta, and Andrei Shleifer, 1999, Corporate ownership around the world, Journal of Finance 54, 471-517.

Madura, Jeff, Allan L. Tucker, and Marilyn Wiley, Marilyn, 1997, Factors affecting returns across stock markets," Global Finance Journal 8, 1-14.

Marsh, Paul, 1979, Equity rights issues and the efficiency of the UK stock market, Journal of Finance 34, 839-862.

Mesler, Donald T., 1986, Warrants. Chicago: Probus.

Mikkelson, Wayne H., and M. Megan Partch, 1986, Valuation effects of security offerings, Journal of Financial Economics 15, 31-60.

Modigliani, Franco, and Merton H. Miller, 1958, The cost of capital, corporation finance and the theory of investment, American Economic Review 48, 261-297.

Modigliani, Franco, and Richard Sutch, 1966, Innovations in interest rate policy, American Economic Review 56, 178-197.

Prowse, Stephen David, 1992, The structure of corporate ownership in Japan, Journal of Finance 42, 1121-1140.

No Author, International Securities Law. London: Euromoney Publications.

Redmayne, Julian, n.d., Equity Warrants. Nestor House, Playhouse Yard: Euromoney Books.

Smith, Jr., Clifford W., 1977, Alternative methods for raising capital: rights versus underwritten offerings, Journal of Financial Economics 5, 273-307.

Tse, Yiu Kuen, 1993, Foreign versus local shares in the Singapore stock market, SES Journal (March), 8-12.

Vogel, Thomas T, Jr., Exchanges sprout in developing nations, Wall Street Journal, November 14, 1995, p. C1.

Wahab, Mahmoud, and Amit Khandwala, 1993, Why not diversify internationally with ADRs? Journal of Portfolio Management 19, 75-82.

Wang, Junbo, and K. C. John Wei, 2006, An analysis of the share price and accounting performance of rights offerings in China, Pacific-Basin Finance Journal, 14, 49–72.

CHAPTER TWO

DEBT SECURITIES

Key Terms

Agency-type risk—risk that occurs when the value of a debt instrument diminishes due to the actions taken by an issuer.

Bankers' acceptance—a draft that orders a particular individual, business, or financial institution to pay a specified amount at a specified time that has been guaranteed (accepted) by a bank

Basis point—0.01% of face value.

Bearer bonds—the identity of the owner is not recorded.

Book—the securities position owned by a firm.

Call money—short-term loans that are repayable at the request of either party.

Capital market—debt instruments with a maturity of one year or longer.

Commercial paper—a short-term unsecured promissory note issued by a corporation.

Conversion ratio—the number of shares received upon the conversion of a convertible bond.

Conversion value—the market value of the shares that would be received if a convertible issue were immediately converted.

Convertible bonds—bonds that can be exchanged for equity in the issuer of the bonds.

Coupons—attachments to bearer bonds that can be submitted to the paying agent to collect interest.

Crisis at maturity—the risk that a large payment due at the maturity of a bond will trigger a default.

Current yield—the annual coupon rate divided by the market price of the bond.

Debentures—unsecured corporate bonds.

Default risk—risk that the issuer will not pay the principal or interest when due or will fail to fulfill other terms of the indenture.

Discount—a bond selling below face value, or, the sale of a non-interest bearing instrument at less than face value.

Eurobonds—trans-national bonds.

Exchangeable bonds—bonds that can be exchanged for the equity of a firm other than the issuer.

Face value—the principal payment due at the maturity of the bond issue, or, for bonds without a fixed maturity, their stated value. See also maturity value or par value.

Federal funds—deposits at the U.S. Federal Reserve available for immediate transfer between financial institutions.

Fiscal agent—a financial institution that handles bond authentication and distribution and the duties of the paying agent.

Flat—a bond that does not trade plus accrued interest because the issuer has defaulted.

Forward interest rate—the interest rate for a period beginning at $t > 0$.

General obligation bonds—bonds backed by the "full faith and credit" of the issuer so that the issuer has promised to do whatever is necessary to repay the bonds.

Immunized—a portfolio whose value does not change with changes in interest rates.

Indenture—the agreement between the bondholders and the issuer of a bond.

Interest rate risk—risk due to fluctuations in the value of a bond due to changing interest rates.

Islamic banking—the adherence to banking practices that conform to the requirements of Islam.

Liquidity risk (trading)—risk that an issue cannot be sold readily at a price close to the current price.

Liquidity hypothesis of term structure—the view that because risk-averse investors prefer to invest in short-term instruments to avoid interest rate risk issuers of long term bonds have to pay a liquidity premium.

Market segmentation hypothesis—see preferred habitat hypothesis.

Maturity value—see face value.

Money markets—the debt market for instruments that have a maturity of less than one year.

Municipal bonds—bonds issues by U.S. states, subdivisions (counties, cities, water districts, conservation districts, and scores of others) or compacts of states (Port of New York Authority).

Negotiable certificate of deposit—a certificate issued by a bank that represents a deposit that can be transferred from one investor to another.

Par value—see face value.

Paying agent—a financial institution that receives the interest and principal payments from the issuer and pays it to the bondholders.

Plus accrued interest—the purchaser pays the seller the negotiated price plus interest from the last interest payment date to the settlement date.

Preferred habitat hypothesis—the hypothesis that because investors and borrowers have a preference for particular maturities along the term structure risk premiums are needed to induce investors and borrowers to shift from one part of the yield curve to another.

Premium—a bond selling above face value. (Note that there are a number of other definitions of this term in other contexts in finance.)

Protective covenants—terms of a bond indenture that prohibit certain actions by the issuer.

Pure expectations hypothesis—forward interest rates are determined exclusively by expectations concerning future interest rates.

Raba—the charging of interest.

Registered—the identity of the owner is recorded on the books of the registrar.

Registrar—a firm, usually a financial institution, that maintains the ownership records of a securities issue and is responsible for checking that the number of shares received by the new owner equals the number of shares supplied by the old owner.

Repurchase agreement (repos)—a contract in which one party sells securities to a counterparty in exchange for an immediate payment with an agreement to repurchase the securities at a specified time and for a fixed price.

Revenue bonds—bonds whose interest and principal payments are contingent on having sufficient revenues from a specific revenue source.

Reverse repurchase agreement—a contract in which one party buys securities from a counterparty in exchange for an immediate payment with an agreement to resell the securities at a specified time and for a fixed price.

***Samurai* bonds**—bonds issued in Japanese capital markets using Japanese investment bankers and denominated in JPY.

Security—an asset on which a particular creditor has a claim prior to the claims of other creditors.

Serial bonds—bond issues in which a portion of the bonds mature each year.

***Shogun* bonds**—the market for USD-denominated bonds in Japan.

Sinking fund—a provision of a bond indenture calling for (1) the retirement of a portion of the bonds prior to maturity either by call or through open market purchases, or (2) the accumulation over the life of an issue of funds sufficient to retire the bonds at maturity.

Sovereign risk—risk that a country will not honor contractual obligations concerning its debt.

Spot interest rate—the interest rate for a period beginning at t = 0.

Straight-debt value of a convertible—the value of a convertible bond without the conversion feature.

Structured repos—the U.S. term for repos with maturities longer than overnight.

Subordinated debentures—bonds having claims on a firm's assets and earnings that are inferior to those of other bonds.

Term bonds—a bond issue in which the entire principal must be repaid at a future date.

Term repo—the European term for repos with maturities longer than overnight.

Term structure of interest rates—a graph reflecting data for a group of bonds that shows the term to maturity on the horizontal axis and the interest rate on the vertical axis.

Treasury bill—a short term government debt instrument.

Tri-party repo—a repo in which a third party custodian handles the exchange of securities and cash on the purchase date and takes custody of the purchased securities.

Trustee (bonds)—a representative of the bondholders who insures that the issuer fulfills its obligations.

Yankee bonds—domestic-currency-denominated nondomestic bonds.

Zero-coupon bonds—bonds that are initially sold at a discount and do not pay interest.

THIS CHAPTER is divided into three parts. In the first, we describe a number of issues related to debt securities including:
- Risks faced by debt investors,
- The term structured of interest rates
- Rating of debt securities, and
- Islamic banking.

Then, we describe the most common types of money market instruments, namely:
- Government issues such as Treasury bills,

> - Negotiable certificates of deposit,
> - Commercial paper,
> - Repurchase agreements,
> - Call money,
> - U.S. Federal funds, and
> - Bankers' acceptances.
>
> Next, we describe bond markets including:
> - Bond characteristics,
> - Convertible and exchangeable bonds,
> - How bonds are traded in secondary markets,
> - Call features,
> - U.S. municipal bonds,
> - Global bond markets, and
> - The use of auctions in connections with debt securities.

1. Introduction

Debt is often considered to be less risky than stocks. However, debt interments carry significant risks. In fact, a portfolio comprising only bonds carries a higher risk than a portfolio with 50% stocks and 50% bonds. Understanding the risk associated with bonds is critical for effective investment.

2. Risks faced by debt investors

Investors in debt instruments face many types of risk.

Interest rate risk is the risk of capital loss due to fluctuations in interest rates. The value of debt instruments varies inversely with interest rates. In other words an increase in interest rates decreases the value of debt while a decrease in interest rates increases the value of debt.

Default risk is the risk that the issuer will not pay the principal or interest when due or will fail to fulfill other terms of the indenture. Default risk is often highest at the maturity of an issue because an issuer can make small interest payments but cannot make a large principal payment.

Liquidity risk is risk that an issue cannot be sold readily at a price close to the current price.

Agency-type risk is the risk that occurs when the value of a debt instrument diminishes due to the actions taken by an issuer. Issuers may undertake mergers that substantially change the industries in which a firm operates, increasing operating risk. In addition, the higher debt/equity ratios often associated with acquisitions may increase financial risk. Investors typically try to anticipate agency risks. To the extent that they are successful investors can either write contracts that limit the actions of issuers to reduce agency risks or investors can demand extra interest to compensate for these risks. Nevertheless, issuers sometimes take unforeseen actions so that investors sustain a loss for which they had not anticipated and for which they were not compensated. Box 2-1 describes an actual case in which agency risk led to capital losses for bondholders.

Sovereign risk is the risk that a country will not honor contractual obligations concerning its debt. Sovereign risk is unique because there is generally no mechanism to force countries to fulfill their promises.

3. The term structure of interest rates

3.1. Introduction

For a group of bonds that are similar except for maturity, the term structure of interest rates is a graph that shows the term to maturity on the horizontal axis and the interest rate on the vertical axis. The term structure of interest rates can take on a variety of shapes. In 1982 the term structure was upward sloping while in 1981 it was downward sloping.[1] Care must be taken in constructing the term structure since the yield on particular bonds can reflect more than just the time value of money. Other factors that might affect the computed yield-to-maturity include default risk and whether a bond is callable. As a result yield curves are most commonly calculated for government issues where default risk is low and other features of the bonds tend to be similar.

---

[1] Bloomberg provides online yield curves for the US, Japan and several other countries at its web site: http://www.bloomberg.com.

> **Box 2-1. The Marriott Corporation**
>
> In 1993 The Marriott Corporation, which operated a variety of business related to the hotel industry, reorganized into two companies. Marriott International's businesses were involved in lodging and facilities management, food services, senior living services, and distribution. It had revenues of about 7.4 billion USD, operating profits of 314 million USD, and net income of 145 million USD. Host Marriott owned hotels and other real estate. It had revenues of 1.7 billion USD, operating profits of 148 million USD, and a net loss of 66 million USD. Management proposed spinning off Marriott International, which represented almost 80% of the value of the pre-spin-off firm, with Marriott Corporation retaining most of its debt. The projected interest coverage of Marriott Corporation would have declined from 2.6 times prior to the spinoff to 1.3 times after the spinoff. On the day that the spin-off was announced Moody's downgraded the rating on the firm's senior debt.
>
> Subsequently, the value of Marriott Corporation's common stock increased by 80.6 million USD and the value of Marriott Corporation's debt declined by 194.6 million USD. Hence, the spinoff destroyed value overall, but there was a wealth transfer from the bondholders to the stockholders. Despite the fact that the bond indenture provided no protection against this type of reorganization, the bondholders filed a number of suites designed to stop the proposed spin-off. The bondholders were eventually successful in forcing Marriott to revise the terms of the proposed spin-off in a number of ways including swapping the old bonds for new bonds with longer maturities and higher interest payments.
>
> Source: Robert Parrino, 1997, Spinoffs and wealth transfers: the Marriott case, Journal of Financial Economics 43, 241-274.

3.2 Theories of the term structure of interest rates

There are three major hypotheses concerning the determinants of the term structure: the expectations hypothesis, the liquidity premium hypothesis, and the market segmentation hypothesis.

3.2.1. Expectations hypothesis

Spot interest rates are interest rates that begin at time t = 0. An interest rate that begins at time t > 0 is called a **forward interest rate**. According to the **pure expectations hypothesis** forward interest rates are determined exclusively by expectations concerning future interest rates. An upward-sloping term structure indicates that future interest rates are expected to increase and a downward-sloping term structure indicates that future interest rates are expected to decrease. Current forward rates are unbiased expectations of future spot rates. Suppose that investors have a choice at time 0 of either purchasing a bond that matures at time t or of purchasing a series of one-year bonds and rolling over each bond at maturity. Let $_tr_{t+n}$ be the interest rate with spot rates indicated by t = 0 and forward rates by t > 0. The interest rate is from the time of the first subscript to the second subscript. Then, if the pure expectations hypothesis holds, we expect that

$$(1 + {_0r_n})^n = (1 + {_0r_1})(1 + {_1r_2})(1 + {_2r_3}) \ldots (1 + {_{n-1}r_n})$$

For n = 5 we would have

$$(1 + {_0r_5})^5 = (1 + {_0r_1})(1 + {_1r_2})(1 + {_2r_3})(1 + {_3r_4})(1 + {_4r_5}).$$

Various version of the expectations hypothesis have been tested. Sarno et al. (2007) test whether the long-term rate is determined by the market's expectation of the short-term rate plus a risk premium. These authors reject the expectations hypothesis for all maturities. Most early tests, beginning with Macaulay (1938), find no empirical support for the expectations hypothesis. In fact, much of the time changes in interest rates have been the opposite of that predicted by the expectations hypothesis. More recent evidence has been mixed. Meiselman (1966) finds empirical support for the pure expectations hypothesis. Santomero (1975) also finds support for the expectations hypothesis, but with a substantial liquidity premium. Nelson (1972) and McCulloch (1975) do not find support for the expectations hypothesis. Froot (1989) reports that while the expectations hypothesis does not hold for short rates, it does hold for long rates. Despite the mixed evidence, most scholars and practitioners who study interest rates believe that the yield curve incorporates the market's expectations concerning future interest rates.

Forward rates are not particularly accurate predictors of future spot rates (see Culbertson, 1957; Fama, 1976). Fama (1979) concludes that a simple prediction that the future spot rate will be the same as the current spot rate is a better prediction than that the future spot rate will equal the current implied forward rate. Culbertson (1957) reaches a similar conclusion. Nevertheless, investors may find the information obtained by examining forward rates useful. Investors are often faced with the alternative of locking in a particular rate over a given horizon or of investing in a series of shorter term instruments over the same horizon. Which alternative investors prefer depends on the investors' view of future interest rates relative to those of the market as reflected in the term structure.

3.2.2. Liquidity hypothesis of term structure

Hicks (1939) was an early proponent of the **liquidity hypothesis**, the view that risk-averse investors prefer to invest in short-term instruments because long-term bonds have greater interest rate risk than short-term bonds. Issuers of long term bonds would have to pay a liquidity premium to induce investors to hold these more risky instruments. Hence, if the liquidity premium hypothesis holds, expected forward rates are an upwardly biased expectation of future spot rates. This implies that the expected return from holding a series of one-year bonds is less than the expected return from holding a single bond over the same time horizon.

3.2.3. Market segmentation and preferred habitat hypothesis

Culbertson (1957) developed the **market segmentation hypothesis**, which argues that individuals and institutions prefer to lend short because this increases their flexibility to meet unexpected contingencies. Borrowers, on the other hand, prefer long maturities to decrease refinancing risk. In this view neither investors nor borrowers are willing to shift their horizon. Hence, speculators are needed to offset differences between long and short demand by borrowing short and lending long, but these speculators will need to be compensated for the risk they incur by receiving risk premiums on the bonds they purchase.

Modigliani and Sutch (1966) developed the **preferred habitat hypothesis**, which asserts that investors and borrowers have a preference for particular maturities. Some borrowers such as manufacturers may be financing long-lived projects, which may be more suited to financing with long-lived bonds rather than, say, by using commercial paper. Insurance companies and pension funds may have obligations with long maturities. Other borrowers such as banks have short-lived liabilities and, therefore, may prefer assets with shorter maturities. Thus, different groups of borrowers and lenders have different preferences concerning the preferred maturities of the instruments they desire. Along some portions of the yield curve supply is likely to be high relative to demand, resulting in lower interest rates, while for other maturities the demand is likely to be high relative to the supply, resulting in relatively high interest rates. The relatively higher interest rates needed to equate supply and demand when there is an excess of demand can be viewed as a positive risk premium. The relatively lower interest rates needed to equate supply and demand when there is an excess of supply can be viewed as negative risk premiums. Hence, according to this hypothesis, the shape of the yield curve is determined at least in part by positive or negative risk premiums needed to induce investors and borrowers to switch out of their preferred habitats. In the preferred habitat hypothesis borrowers and lenders themselves are induced to shift their supply and demand to take advantage of differences in relative risk premiums. Cox, Ingersoll, and Ross (1981) argue that the liquidity hypothesis can be considered a special case of the preferred habitat hypothesis. These two hypotheses along with the market segmentation hypothesis support the idea that the term structure reflects both the time value of money and risk premiums. Fama (1976) provides evidence of the existence of risk premium in interest rates.

4. Ratings

There are many debt issuers in the major capital markets so that most individual and institutional investors are not easily able to assess the quality of each issue. Because of this problem there are a number of firms that specialize in helping investors assess the safety of debt issues by assigning ratings.[1] The USSEC has designated four nationally recognized statistical rating organizations for rating all U.S. corporate bond issues: Moody's, Standard and Poor's, Fitch IBCA, and Duff & Phelps. Moody's began rating bonds in 1909 and Standard and Poor's begun in 1916. Both Moody's and Standard and Poor's rate all taxable publicly issued bonds in the U.S., but Fitch and Duff & Phelps provide ratings only when they are hired by the issuer. Several rating agencies specialize in particular industries. Thomson Bankwatch rates issues of financial institutions and A.M. Best rates insurance companies. IBCA also specialized in the issues of financial institutions prior to its merger with Fitch to form Fitch IBCA.

In 1996 there were three rating agencies in Japan: Nippon Investors Services, Inc., Japan Credit Rating Agency, and Japan Bond Research Institute. The rating agencies provide a simple and easily understood symbol to show an issue's relative credit quality. Rating agencies may rate negotiable certificates of deposit and commercial paper as well as bonds. Debt issuers typically must pay to obtain a Japanese rating.

Standard and Poor's rates bonds as: AAA, AA, A, BBB, BB, B, CCC and C with additional ratings grades for bonds with special characteristics. Rating categories A through CCC are further divided into three categories. Table 2-1 lists Moody's and Standard and Poor's rating categories. The first four categories are called "investment grade" and the remaining categories are "speculative." These terms do not indicate whether these are good investments since that judgment depends on factors such as the risk preferences of the investor and differences in expected returns from one instrument to another. An investment grade rating indicates that S&P has no reason to believe that payments will not be timely.

---

[1] Many of the rating services have web sites: Moody's, http://www.moodys.com/moodys/mdyindex.htm; Standard and Poor's, http://www.standardandpoors.com/ratings/corporates/index.htm; Fitch IBCA, http://www.fitchibca.com/home/frame.html; Duff & Phelps, http://www.dcrco.com/; Thomson Bankwatch, http://www.bankwatch.com/bankw.htm; and A.M. Best, http://www.ambest.com/other.html. The A.M. Best rating system is described at http://www.ambest.com/ratings/preface/pc/contents.htm.

Table 2-1. Rating symbols for long-term debt.

Interpretation	Moody's	Standard and Poor's
INVESTMENT-GRADE RATINGS		
Highest Quality	Aaa	AAA
High Quality	Aa1	AA+
	Aa2	AA
	Aa3	AA-
Strong payment capacity	A1	A+
	A2	A
	A3	A-
Adequate payment capacity	Baa1	BBB+
	Baa2	BBB
	Baa3	BBB-
SPECULATIVE-GRADE RATINGS		
Likely to fulfill obligations, ongoing uncertainty	Ba1	BB+
	Ba2	BB
	Ba3	BB-
High-risk obligations	B1	B+
	B2	B
	B3	B-
Issues are in poor standing (may be in default)	Caa1	CCC+
	Caa2	CCC
	Caa3	CCC-
Have extremely poor prospects	C1	CC
	C2	C
	C3	

Source: Compiled from
http://www.moodys.com/ratings/ratdefs.htm#lttaxable
http://www.standardandpoors.com/ratings/corporates/index.htm.

In 1989 S&P began to rate bonds as to their protection from event risk. An example of event risk is the 1992 restructuring of Marriott Corporation, a firm owning a variety of businesses including hotels and restaurants, into two separate entities (see Box 2-1 for more information). One held the business with the most favorable prospects. The second held the remaining businesses and was obligated for most of the firm's debt. Naturally, the bond's price declined as a result of the reorganization, resulting in an uncompensated transfer of wealth from the bondholders to the equity holders.

Bonds that have a speculative rating are called either junk bonds or, because of their high coupon rates or high current yields, high yield bonds

Historically, in the U.S. speculative grade bonds have been "fallen angels," bonds initially issued with a higher rating, but which had been downgraded because of the issuer's deteriorating credit quality. In 1976 Drexel Burnham Lambert, an investment bank, began to seek out firms to raise new funds using low-rated debt. At the same time Drexel began to develop a secondary market for these bonds. Initially, companies that offered new issues of junk bonds were companies that had previously used bank term loans and other similar sources of financing. By 1983 junk bonds were beginning to become an important source of financing for acquisitions. In the early 1990s there were many defaults of junk bonds, but the market subsequently recovered and remains a major sector of the U.S. corporate bond market.

A study of the efficacy of ratings in the U.S. in predicting subsequent default over the period 1900-1943 concluded that the record was remarkably good.[1] Increased interest rate volatility since the early 1970s has made it more difficult for many issues to sustain their credit quality.

Rating agencies also rate countries or sovereign credits. These sovereign ratings are important because countries are the largest issuers in the international capital markets. Moreover, rating agencies rarely assign a credit rating to a governmental entity or private company located in a country that is higher than the rating received by the country on its own debt.[2] As of

---

[1] Hickman (1958).

[2] Moody's sovereign ceilings for foreign-currency ratings can be found at http://www.moodys.com/repldata/ratings/ratsov.htm.

September 1995 both Moody's and Standard and Poor's rated forty-nine countries. In a general sense these ratings measure the same thing as rating of other issuers: safety of principal and interest payments. The agency examines the country's willingness and ability to honor its external obligations. In dealing with countries willingness is especially important because it is generally not possible for a citizen of one country to enforce a claim against another country. Economic self-interest is one of the most important factors in encouraging countries to pay their debts. Countries that have a history of paying their debts generally have low borrowing costs and easier access to credit markets. A stable government with a history of smooth transfer of power is desirable. Relations with other nations and with the country's own citizens are also important. Important economic factors include: trends in economic growth, diversification of the economy, the current level of external debt, and liquidity factors such as balance-of-payments considerations.

5. Islamic banking

Many practices in modern banking violate commandments of the Shair'ah, Islamic law. The holy book of Islam, the Qur'an, forbids the charging of **raba** or interest. The predominant view among Islamic scholars is that the prohibition against raba bans more than just usury, but also the charging of any fixed or predetermined payment beyond the principal. There is a growing movement to develop alternate banking practices that conform to the requirements of the Shari'ah. The adherence to banking practices that conform to the requirements of Islam is known as **Islamic banking**. The actual implementation and practices allowed differ from country to country, but share many elements. Lenders must share in the risks and well as the rewards of activities financed by loans. Hence, depositors are not promised fixed returns, but share in the profits and losses of the bank. The banks, in turn, do not make loans requiring the payment of fixed interest. Instead they enter into various types of partnerships and joint ventures with their clients.[1] According to Bilal (1999)

---

[1] A bibliography on topics related to Islamic banking, links to financial institutions following Islamic practices is at this web address:

Islamic "instruments give more importance to the valuation of anticipated profits than to collateral." Dow Jones sponsors the Dow Jones Islamic Market Index, which includes 600 companies from 30 countries (including the US). Companies included in the index do not provide goods and services that violate Shari'ah law. These forbidden products include alcoholic beverages, pork and tobacco products, defense companies, hotels, casinos, cinemas, and non-Islamic financial services. The index also excludes companies with high debt ratios. Not all countries or Islamic investors eschew all of these goods and services. Cigarette companies trade on the Jakarta Stock Exchange and casinos stocks trade on the Kuala Lumpur Stock Exchange.

6. Money markets

All modern financial centers have money markets that allow financial and nonfinancial institutions to obtain funds to meet short-term liquidity needs and to invest surplus funds on a short-term basis. In the largest financial centers such as the U.S. and Japan the money markets include instruments denominated both in local currency and also in other major currencies.

6.1. Non-domestic money market instruments

There are many types of money market instruments traded in financial markets throughout the world. Similar types of instruments are traded in major financial centers, but the particular instruments that are most actively traded depend largely on government policies, regulations, and taxes, or on historical developments within each country. There have been active money markets in the U.S. for many years. In the U.S. the principle wholesale interbank market is the Federal funds market, in part, because there are no reserve requirements for Federal funds. While there has been a small money market in Japan for many years, its size and diversity has grown rapidly

---

http://islamic-finance.net/. Chapter 4 of the book Interest-free Commercial Banking by A.L.M. Gafoor can be found at: http://www.noord.bart.nl/~abdul/chap4.html.

since 1985 when the Bank of Japan began to establish new money markets and to relax requirements concerning denominations, maturities, and market participation.

6.1.1. Treasury bills

Many countries have active markets for short-term government debt instruments. More than 500 billion USDs of U.S. Treasury bills are outstanding. Treasury bills have a maximum maturity of one year when they are issued and are sold at a discount from face value. The difference between the face value and the sale price represents interest so separate payment of interest. The minimum purchase amount is 10,000 USD with multiples of 5,000 USD thereafter.

There is a large over-the-counter secondary market in U.S. Treasury bills. In the U.S. there are about 1,700 registered U.S. government securities broker-dealers, including 250 depository institutions and 1,450 securities firms, but the majority of trading volume is accounted for by thirty-seven primary dealers. Brokers handle much of the trading even between dealers. Brokers act only as agents and allow the dealers to trade with each other anonymously. Brokers provide dealers with screens for disseminating quotes and trading information. Broker commissions are negotiable but might range from 12.50 USD per 1 million USD of three-month treasury notes to about 40 USD per 1 million USD for notes and bonds. The dealers trade 22 to 23 hours each day, five days a week, but 95 percent of the trading takes place during New York trading hours.

There are also active markets for U.S. Treasury bills in Tokyo and London. The trading day begins in Tokyo at about 7:00 a.m. Tokyo time. Many institutions holding inventories of U.S. Treasury bills pass their **book**, the record of and responsibility for securities positions, to London at about 16:00 Tokyo time. These positions are then managed in London until near the end of the trading day, say at 13:00 London time (8:00 New York time) when the book is passed to New York. At the end of the trading day in New York the book is passed back to Japan and the cycle starts again.

The market for Treasury bills issued by the Japanese government began in 1986 when bills of six months' maturity were issued. Primary issues are in minimum denominations of 10 million JPY and purchase of these issues is restricted to financial institutions, insurance companies, and securities companies. In addition, corporations, but not individuals, can participate in the secondary market.

6.1.2. Negotiable certificates of deposit

Negotiable certificates of deposit (CDs) are financial instruments issued by commercial banks in exchange for time deposits. CDs can be transferred from one investor to another. CDs are traded domestically within many countries and in international markets. The instruments first began trading in 1961 when the First National City Bank of New York announced that it would begin issuing negotiable certificates of deposit in large denominations and that a major U.S. government securities dealer had agreed to make a market in these instruments. Other large U.S. banks quickly followed City Bank's lead. Banks use this market to purchase funds to finance loan and investment demand. An active secondary market quickly developed and flourishes today. This market allows corporations and other with large amounts of short-term funds to buy these negotiable certificates of deposit and resell them after a short holding period.

Interest rates increased in the first part of the 1960s so U.S. banks could no longer issue CDs because market interest rates rose above the rates that depositary institutions were permitted to offer at that time.[1] To avoid these ceilings, U.S. banks began issuing CDs in London in 1966. These proved so popular that banks in other countries began issuing their own CDs. In Japan any bank that is eligible to accept deposits can issue negotiable certificates of deposit. Maturities range from two weeks to two years. British banks began issuing GPB CDs in 1968 and Singapore and Hong Kong followed with local currency CDs in 1975 and 1977, respectively. In Australia a change in Australian reserve requirements in 1988 resulted in an increase in the usage of negotiable certificates of deposit as the primary money market instrument and a corresponding reduction in bankers' acceptances.

---

[1] A deposit is a loan from the depositor. Banks induce customers to make these loans in the form of deposits by offering interest and/or by facilitating payments.

6.1.3. Commercial paper

Commercial paper is a short-term unsecured promissory note issued by a corporation. Commercial paper sold at a discount through dealers makes it possible for nonfinancial corporations to raise funds directly from investors without going through banks. Large banks obtain funds at rates comparable to commercial paper rates so that after adding fees to cover their costs and profits, banks loads are more costly than commercial paper loans. Firms with the highest credit ratings issue most commercial paper so that no security is required. **Security** refers to assets on which a particular creditor has a claim prior to the claims of other creditors. Firms that do not have high credit ratings themselves may be able to transfer sufficient assets to a subsidiary to give it a high credit rating. The subsidiary can then issue commercial paper. Most commercial paper is sold through dealers who purchase the paper from the issuer and resell it to investors. Dealer fees amount to about 10 basis points per year or about 1 basis point for 36 days.

The largest commercial paper dealers are investment banking firms such as Merrill Lynch and Goldman Sachs and investment banking subsidiaries of commercial banks such as CitiCorp and Bankers Trust, a U.S. bank specializing in derivatives. The growth of the commercial paper market demonstrates that many firms can obtain funds more cheaply by directly accessing the money markets than through the banking system.

Only very large firms issue commercial paper directly without going through dealers. In the U.S. finance subsidiaries of major durable goods manufacturers use commercial paper to raise funds to finance the promissory notes received from their customers when the buy new automobiles and other company products. The three largest issuers of commercial paper in the U.S. are General Motors Acceptance Corporation, General Electric Capital, and Ford Motor Credit. There are about 125 direct issuers of commercial paper. Distribution costs including agent fees, rating fees, backup credit fees, and the like might amount to only 15 basis points for larger commercial paper issuers. In the U.S., at the time it is initially placed, commercial paper normally carries maturities of from 30 to 270 days. Maturities of longer than 270 days must be registered with the USSEC, which makes it too costly and cumbersome for issuing firms. Settlement for commercial paper transactions is on the same day as the transaction and more than 40 percent of the commercial paper issued in the U.S. is in book-entry form.

Borrowers frequently issue new paper to pay off their maturing issues. Credit lines from banks may be required to insure that there will be sufficient liquidity if the firm cannot refinance maturing paper by selling new commercial paper. This occurred in 1970 when the default of Penn Central railroad on 82 million USD of commercial paper temporarily disputed the market. The bank lines that firms use to insure liquidity do not guarantee the credit worthiness of the issuer and these letters of credit generally have "material adverse conditions" clauses which allow them to be withdrawn if the issuer's financial condition changes materially. When Mercury Finance was accused of falsifying its books and defaulted on 19 million USD of commercial paper, its banks withdrew lines of credit of more than 500 million USD.[1]

In the U.S. companies without the highest credit ratings have been able to issue commercial paper using several methods to provide credit enhancements. The issuer can pay a fee to a bank to obtain a letter of credit that cannot be withdrawn. Lenders then focus on the creditworthiness of the bank. Since most U.S. banks do not have a sufficiently high credit rating to issue these letters of credit, most are issued by non-U.S. banks. Insurance firms also issue indemnity bonds that permit the issuance of letters of credit.

The U.S. commercial paper market is also open at least to some extent to non-U.S. firms. In mid-1998, BankAmerica arranged a $200 million USD commercial paper program for a wholly-owned subsidiary of China National Metals & Minerals Import & Export Corporation, China's main company for importing and exporting metals and minerals for the last 48 years. Bank of America issued a letter of credit to support the commercial paper program.[2]

---

[1] Wall Street Journal Interactive Edition, 1997, Mercury finance's chief resigns amid serious financial squeeze, February 3.

[2] For additional information see:
http://www.bankamerica.com/news/news422.html.

While the U.S. commercial paper market is the largest there are also active commercial paper markets in other countries such as Japan.[1] The minimum denomination is 100 million JPY and maturities range from two weeks to nine months. To be eligible for issuing commercial paper companies must meet strict financial requirements related to net worth and liquidity ratios. More than 500 firms are eligible to issue commercial paper in Japan, but fewer than half of these have done so.

Some U.S. firms issue commercial paper in the U.S. and at the same time issue USD-dominated commercial paper in the Euro commercial paper market. The majority of Euro commercial paper is denominated in USD though there are also significant amounts denominated in other currencies such as the ECU and JPY. Maturities in the Euro market are typically longer than in the U.S., say 60 to 180 days, and because of the longer maturities there is a more active secondary market. The credit quality of the Euro market has been lower than that for the U.S. market and this has been reflected in a higher level of defaults.

6.1.4. Repurchase agreements

In a **repurchase agreement** (repo) one party sells securities to a counterparty in exchange for an immediate payment with an agreement to repurchase the securities at a specified time and for a fixed price. A **reverse repurchase agreement** involves an initial purchase with an agreement for a subsequent sale. The economic effect of a repurchase agreement is the same as a collateralized loan, but there may be important legal differences if, say, one party files for bankruptcy protection. In evaluating repos it is important to look at both the quality of the securities that are the subject of the repo and the credit standing of the counterparty. Due to regulatory and legal factors that encourage repos, the French repo market began in 1994.[2] French repos use a floating rate index, which is a weighted average of overnight interbank rates, published daily by the bank of France. There is also an active market in transforming floating-rates into fixed rates and vice

---

[1] For an announcement by Merrill Lynch of a commercial paper program in Japan see: http://www.ml.com/woml/press_release/19980302-1.htm.
[2] http://theotcspace.files.wordpress.com/2011/11/003-the-repo-market.pdf

versa. The repo market began in the U.K. in 1996. For many years the Japanese government bond market was inefficient due to lack of an active repo market. But beginning in 1995 the government has encouraged the development of a repo market. There is an active repo market in Japan (called gensaki) which is open to corporations, but not individuals. The minimum transaction size is 10 million yen, but the typical transaction size is 100 million yen. In Germany securities lending and repo transactions are made in government securities, bank bonds, and government bonds of OECD countries. Contracts are most often for one week to three months.

Some trading platforms allow repos to be traded electronically and anonymously and cleared through LCH.Clearnet Ltd's central clearing product, RepoClear.

Historically, most repos have been overnight. If a trader buys an option and hedges it by buying the underlying bond, a repo can be used to finance the bond purchase. The advantage of a repo over straight borrowing is that the repo is collateralized, providing protection from counterparty credit risk. More recently, an active market for longer-maturity repos, called **structured** (in the U.S.) or **term** (in Europe) **repos**, has emerged. Because of the longer-term risk exposure, the structured repo market is limited to firms rated double A or above.

The **tri-party repo** in which a third party custodian handles the exchange of securities and cash on the purchase date and takes custody of the purchased securities peaked in 2008 at about 2.8 trillion USD. The custodian transfers securities that have been agreed to as acceptable to the buyer into a segregated account with title vested in the buyer. The custodian provides services such as daily mark-to-market, cross-currency valuations, and determinations as to whether margins are in excess of deficit. The custodian unwinds the transaction on the repurchase date. Tri-party repos address an important issue of risk in that in standard or "hold in custody" repo the buyer relies on the seller to protect its interest in the collateral. Tri-party repos relieve the seller of clerical and custodial duties.

6.1.5. Call money

Call money refers to short-term bank loans that are repayable at the request of either party. In the U.S. call money provides an important source of funding for brokerage firms supplying money to their customers for margin purchases. Margin customers sign an agreement allowing the brokerage firms to pledge the customers' securities as collateral for these loans. Rates on call money are reported each day in the Wall Street Journal.

There is an active call market for short-term financing in Japan. All transactions must be handled by one of the nine companies licensed to do so by the Ministry of Finance. Both secured and unsecured transactions are possible. Secured transactions require collateral securities that are eligible for pledging with the Bank of Japan. These securities include government bonds, financing bills, government guaranteed bonds, and bank debentures. The maturities for the secured transactions range from overnight up to six days. Unsecured transactions were first permitted in 1985 and the value of unsecured transactions now exceeds that of the secured transactions.

6.1.6. Federal funds

In the U.S. the Monetary Control Act of 1980 requires banks and a number of other depository institutions that are insured by the U.S. government to maintain reserves representing specified percentages of their deposit liabilities. These reserves may be held in cash, but are most commonly held as deposits in a Federal Reserve bank. These deposits at the Federal Reserve, called **Federal funds**, are available for immediate transfer between financial institutions. Deposits in Federal Reserve banks earn no interest so that banks have an incentive to maintain only the required deposit level. Banks can also borrow Federal funds from other banks that have excess funds. Loans of federal funds between financial institutions are most commonly for one day, i.e., overnight, and can be made either directly from one institution to another or through brokers. No reserve requirements apply to these loans. In some cases the loans are secured using U.S. government securities.

6.1.7. Bankers' acceptances

A banker's acceptance is a Bill of Exchange, a draft that orders a particular individual, business or financial institution to pay a specified amount at a specified time. When the drawee, the person required to make the payment, acknowledges the obligation by writing "Accepted" with appropriate signatures on the front the document becomes an acceptance. Typically, banks accept drafts on behalf of their customers, after which the instrument is called a **bankers' acceptance**.

Bankers' acceptances usually arise from letters of credit in foreign trade. An importer in New York might arrange for the delivery of goods from an exporter in Brazil. After satisfying a U.S. bank of its credit worthiness, the importer obtains a letter of credit from the U.S. bank in favor of the exporter, authorizing the exporter to draw a draft upon the U.S. bank in payment for the goods. The draft may call for payment, say 90 days after arrival of the goods in New York. The importer sends his letter of credit to the exporter. After shipping the goods, the exporter can often borrow funds immediately. The exporter's bank will send the draft along with the shipping documents to its correspondent bank in the U.S. and the correspondent bank will present the draft for acceptance. Once accepted the shipping documents are released and the importer can claim the shipment. The exporter's bank may instruct the correspondent bank to hold the acceptance for it as an investment or to sell the acceptance in the secondary market and credit its account. In any event, whoever owns the acceptance is the party financing the transaction.

6.2. Non-domestic money market instruments

The Eurocurrency market comprises all bank deposits and loans in any nondomestic currency. USD held outside the US and JPY held outside Japan are part of this market. The terminology derives from the origins of these markets in Europe though these markets are now worldwide The five largest Eurocurrency currencies in terms of amounts held outside the domestic market are (beginning with the largest): USD, EUR, JPY, GBP, and CHF. Eurocurrency deposits are actively traded mostly through brokers.

7. Bonds

7.1. Bond characteristics

7.1.1. Bond basics

A bond is a security in which an issuer contractually agrees to make one or more payments to an investor. The agreement between the bondholders and the issuer is called the **indenture**. Some countries allow **bearer bonds**, in which the identity of the owner is not recorded. About 3% of Japanese government bonds are in bearer form. The remaining 97% are **registered**, i.e., the identity of the owner is known. The institution maintaining the ownership records is called the **registrar**. In Japan the Bank of Japan acts as registrar. Some countries allow the principal to be registered while the interest is paid using bearer coupons. Historically, in the U.S. bonds of states and subdivisions of states issued bonds in bearer form, but now all new issues must be in registered form. If a bond is registered the issuer can pay interest and principal payments directly to the owner, though both the issuer and the owner are likely to make and receive payment through banks and brokerage firms. If a bond is held in bearer form, **coupons** are attached to the bond. These are detached when due and submitted by the owner for payment.

Because bondholders are dispersed and do not typically know each other's identity, a **trustee**, is appointed to represent the bondholders. It is the duty of the trustee to enforce the term of the indenture. Besides specifying the rate and dates of interest payments and the timing of principal repayment, bonds often have **protective covenants** that prohibit certain actions by the issuer. The issuer may be prohibited from issuing additional debt, especially debt that has a superior claim, or from paying dividends unless specified financial conditions are met.

We use the terms **face value**, **par value**, and **maturity value** interchangeably to mean the principal payment due at the maturity of the bond issue. The typical amount of the face value differs from bond type to bond type and from country to country. Therefore, for convenience, we take the face value of each bond to be 1,000 units of local currency. Prices for bonds are usually stated in percent of face value so that a price of 94 is

94% of the face value of the bond. Interest rates for bonds typically are also stated in percent of face value at an annualized rate. A 5% bond pays 5% of face value each year, even though actual payments might occur semiannually or quarterly. A **basis point** is 0.01% of face value. If a bonds market yield increases by 50 basis points from 5% the new yield is 5.5%. A bond selling at a **discount** is selling below face value while a bond selling at a **premium** is selling above face value.

Most bonds are **term bonds** in which the entire principal must be repaid at a single future date. Typical maturities of bonds vary substantially from country to country. In the U.S. both the U.S. government and corporations commonly issue bonds with short maturities of one or more years and with longer maturities of 30 years or more. Issues with maturities of 100 years were common in the U.S. in the 19th century and firms such as International Business Machines and Walt Disney issued 100-year bonds in the early 1990s. But in Japan bonds with a maturity of 20 years are called "super long-term coupon bonds."[1]

7.1.2. Interest payments

Most bonds pay interest either annually or semiannually. Typically, German government bonds pay interest on the same day each year, on either the 1st or 20th of the month (or the next business day if it is a holiday). In the U.S. bonds typically pay interest every six months, but the dates on which interest is paid vary from issue to issue. Corporate bonds often have a **paying agent**, a bank that has the responsibility of receiving interest and principal payments from the issuer and disbursing them to the bond owners. Most commonly the interest payments on bonds are set at the time of issue. Floating rate bonds with interest payments determined subsequent to the issue are becoming more common. In the early 1990s the German government issued three floating-rate bonds with quarterly coupon payments of three-month LIBOR or three-month DMG minus 20 basis points. LIBOR is the London Interbank Offer Rate, the rate at which funds are exchanged between banks in London. **Zero-coupon bonds** are sold initially at a discount and do not pay interest. Zero-coupon bonds may

---

[1] Yamamoto (1993).

present a problem for U.S. taxpayers because the U.S. government taxes part of the discount each year even though it is not received until maturity.

7.1.3. Call features

There are two distinct types of bond calls. One involves the call of an entire issue and the other involves a call of only selected bonds. Commonly an entire issue cannot be called until several years after issuance. The call price may be par, but if the issue has not been outstanding too long it is likely to be greater than par. The floating rate bonds issued by the German government were callable in one case two years after issuance and in another five years after issuance. No other German government bonds have call features. Issuers prefer callable bonds because they can refinance if interest rates decline. Investors take the opposite view. Sometimes bonds are callable under certain circumstances but not under others. An issue might be callable in case of a merger, but not simply to take advantage of lower interest rates. Also, calls of an entire issue, which we are discussing here, are typically different than calls for sinking fund purposes described next.

A second type of call involving only a part of an issue is designed to prevent "**crisis at maturity**." If at maturity there happen to be a recession or crisis such as a war, it might be difficult to refinance the issue. Bond professionals have developed several ways of dealing with the potential for a crisis at maturity. One approach is to have a **sinking fund** provision. Historically, in the U.S. issuers would simply buy U.S. government bonds or similar instruments each year and hold these in an account so that by the time the bonds matured the bond portfolio would be of sufficient size to retire the debt. Today the typical procedure is for the issuer to repurchase a portion of the issue each year. If the bonds are selling at a discount the issuer simply buys the bonds in the open market. Otherwise the bonds can usually be called at face value. The specific bonds called are determined by lot so that an investor holding a portfolio of the bonds could expect to have a number of bonds called each year approximately equal to a pro rata portion of each year's call.

7.2. Beyond plain vanilla bonds

7.2.1. Convertible and exchangeable bonds

Some bonds can be surrendered to the issuer in return for equity. **Exchangeable bonds** can be exchanged for the equity of a firm other than the issuer. Dart & Kraft has an issue that can be exchanged for shares of Minnesota Mining and Manufacturing. General Cinema has an issue that can be exchanged for shares of both R.J. Reynolds and Sea-Land Corporation. **Convertible bonds** can be surrendered for equity in the issuer of the bonds. Alaska Air Group has an issue maturing in 2014 with 6.875% coupons convertible into 29.762 shares of common stock for each 1,000 USD of face value. 29.762 is the **conversion ratio**, which is the number of shares received upon conversion. The conversion price is $1,000/29.762 = 33.60$ USD per share. Suppose that the market price of the underlying shares is 15.875 USD. The **conversion value** is the market value of the shares that would be received if the issue were immediately converted, i.e., in this case $29.762 \times 15.875 = 472.50$. Stated as a percent of face value the conversion value is 47.25. The bond's **straight-debt value of a convertible** is its value if it were not convertible. In determining the straight value factors such as the credit rating of the issuer and the amount of debt senior to this issue must be taken into account. One way to determine the straight value is to examine the value of comparable nonconvertible bonds. We obtained a straight value of 78 for this bond from the Value Line Convertibles Survey.

The minimum value of a convertible bond is the greater of its (1) conversion value, or (2) straight value. Thus, since 78 is greater than 47.25, the minimum value of this Alaska Air bond is 78. The actual market price of this bond was 85.

7.2.2. Secured bonds and debentures

Another way of classifying corporate bonds is by the type of collateral offered. In the U.S. mortgage bonds have a claim on specific assets of the firm with first mortgage bonds having a superior claim to second mortgage bonds and so forth. Unsecured corporate bonds are called **debentures**. Debentures can also be issued with varying degrees of seniority.

Subordinated debentures have and inferior claim to interest and principal payments. In Japan mortgage bonds are issued under the Secured Bond Trust Law and there are nineteen valid types of mortgages, including mortgages on real estate and on the general assets of the firm. General mortgage bonds have been issued by utilities such as Nippon Telegraph and Telephone Company. Both nonfinancial and financial corporations are allowed to issue debentures in Japan.

7.2.3. Index bonds

In 1997, the U.S. government auctioned its first issue of inflation-adjusted bonds. The issue comprised 7 billion USD of ten-year notes. The securities have a stated rate of interest that does not change over the life of the issue. The principal value is adjusted semiannually for inflation by multiplying the initial face value by an index ratio. The index used is the U.S. City Average All Items Consumer Price Index for All Urban Consumers published by the U.S. Department of Labor (CPI). The ratio is calculated by dividing the CPI on the original issue date by its value on a given valuation date. The inflation adjustment to the principal is not payable until maturity, at which time the holder will receive the greater of the inflation-adjusted principal or the initial par value. Semiannual interest payments are a fixed percentage of the adjusted principal so that the interest payment changes to reflect inflation.

7.2.4. U.S. municipal bonds

In the U.S. issues of any state or any entity created by a state (such as cities, counties, school districts, water districts, airport authorities, etc.) are called **municipal bonds**. Interest payments on municipal bonds are generally exempt from U.S. Federal income tax. **General obligation** bonds are backed by the "full faith and credit" of the issuer. In other words the issuer agrees to do what is necessary to repay the bonds. States, cities, counties and the like must continue to operate even if they cannot pay their debts. So remedies in the case of default may be painful for the debt holders.

In addition to general obligation bonds, municipalities issue **revenue bonds**, bonds whose interest and principal payments are contingent on having sufficient revenues from a specific revenue source. These bonds are used to finance many kinds of facilities including roads, bridges, tunnels, airports, and utilities such as sewers, electric distribution, water, etc. In some cases specific tax revenues are pledged to pay off the issue. The State of Alabama pledged its sales tax revenue to pay some of its bond issues. These bonds were given a high rating because the safety of the revenue was high and the size of the revenue in relation to the issue size was also high.

In the U.S. municipal bonds deal with the potential for crisis at maturity in another way. Municipal bonds are generally not term bonds. Instead they are **serial bonds** in which a portion of the bonds mature each year. In other words, if an issue of 20,000,000 USD is sold in say 2000, some of the issue would have matures in 2001, some in 2002, and so forth. Investors can purchase bonds with a maturity that matches their investment horizon. Banks typically purchase the shorter maturities while individuals or other investors who are fully-taxed for income tax purposes purchase the longer maturity. Box 2-2 describes the largest default of municipal bonds in U.S. history.

Box 2-2. Washington Public Power Supply System

The Washington Public Power Supply System known as Woops initiated work on five nuclear power plants with an initial projected cost of about 8 billion USD. Each plant was financed separately and the financing for plants 1, 2, and 3 was guaranteed by a U.S. government agency. The first three plants were almost complete when Woops announced that its funds were insufficient to complete the projects. Moreover, Woops decided to abandon plants 4 and 5, which had already cost more than 2 billion USD, because they had become uneconomic. The bondholders for plants 4 and 5 expected to receive payment from 88 utilities that had entered into contracts with Woops to pay for the plants whether or not they received any electricity. But Washington State's highest court ruled that these contracts were unenforceable because the utilities lacked the authority to enter into the contracts. As a result of this decision Woops defaulted, becoming the largest municipal default in U.S. history.

See: Seligman (1989) and Sitzer, Noe, and Perko (1994).

7.3. Bond markets

7.3.1. Bond trading

Most secondary market trading of bonds is in over the counter. In the U.S. there is almost no trading of either government or corporate bonds on exchanges. Seventy-five percent of Bundesobligationen, five year notes issued by the Federal Republic of Germany, are traded over-the-counter. About 95 percent of secondary market trading in Japanese government bonds takes place over-the-counter. There are different ways of handling interest when trading bonds. Most often bonds trade **plus accrued interest**. The buyer pays the agreed upon price plus accrued interest from the last interest payment to trade settlement date. Then the buyer receives interest from the last interest payment date to the current interest payment date from the issuer. Netting the interest paid from the interest received leaves the bondholder with the correct amount of interest. There are exceptions to this way of trading. German government bonds trade this way most of the time, but the method of trading changes near interest payment dates. Near a coupon payment date an ex-coupon date is established. A bond that trades and settles in the ex-coupon period trades with negative accrued interest. In other words, the seller retains the coupon and receives the purchase price less interest from the settlement date to the next interest payment date. Trades made before the ex-date that settle after the ex-date can be made with either positive or negative accrued interest. Most international investors prefer to settle this latter type of trade on a negative interest basis to avoid risk due to failure of the seller to remit the interest payment when received. Defaulted bonds are another exception to the practice of trading bonds plus accrued interest. Bonds that are in default typically are traded **flat** so that only the agreed upon price is exchanged. All interest payments paid by the issuer after the settlement date, including any back interest, are the property of the buyer.

7.3.2. Global markets

It is now common for issuers to raise funds in multiple countries. Historically, a company headquartered in one country might sell bonds in another. A more recent trend has been for a firm to offer its bonds in more than one country simultaneously. These are called **global offerings**.[1] Another recent innovation has been the issuance of bonds with the principle payable in one currency and the interest in another.

Bonds issued in a country by nonresidents are called **foreign bonds**. One part of this market is for domestic-currency-denominated nondomestic bonds. Countries often make a distinction between domestic and nondomestic bond issues in terms of factors such as regulatory requirements and taxes. There may be differences in who can purchase the bonds, in the sizes of the issues that are allowed, and in information reporting requirements. After World War II many nonresidents issued bonds in the U.S. These bonds are called **Yankee bonds**. In recent years the market share of these USD-denominated bonds has declined. The largest market for foreign bonds is Switzerland. This does not mean that the Swiss are the largest holders of these bonds, but simply that more of these bonds are denominated in SWF than in other currencies. Since the SWF is a stable currency, issuers and investors might prefer to issue bonds in SWF rather than in their own currency. Nonresidents issue bonds in the Japanese capital markets using Japanese investment bankers and denominating the bonds in JPY. These bonds are called **samurai bonds**.[2] The Asian Development Bank issued the first samurai bonds in 1970.[3] The International Bank for Reconstruction and Development (e.g., the World Bank) issued samurai bonds in 1971[4] and Australia followed in 1972. The first corporation to issue these bonds was Sears in 1979. There are also important markets for nondomestic bonds denominated in local currency in the U.K., Germany, and the Netherlands.

Another type of foreign bond is the bond issued in a country by nonresidents, but in a nonlocal currency. The market for USD-denominated bonds in Japan (**shogun bonds**) began in 1985 with an issue by the World Bank. The first private issuer of shogun bonds was Southern California Edison Company in 1985. An easing of Japanese government

---

[1] Karmin and Zuckerman (1998).

[2] Packer and Reynolds (1997).

[3] The web site for the Asian development Bank is: http://www.adb.org/.

[4] For a discussion of the global bond issues of the World Bank see: http://www.worldbank.org/foddr/global.htm.

regulations for larger issuers helped the growth of the market. The U.S. government also allowed U.S. corporations to issue bonds outside the U.S. in bearer form.

Eurobonds are trans-national issues typically underwritten by an international investment banking syndicate. Most Eurobonds are in bearer form with interest paid annually. Eurobonds are generally free of withholding tax, but if one is withheld the issuer has to increase the interest payment to offset the tax. Some Eurobond issues have a **paying agent** and a **trustee**. The paying agent receives the interest and principal payments from the issuer and pays them to the bondholders. The trustee represents the bondholders and makes sure that the issuer fulfills its obligations. Other issues have only a **fiscal agent** who handles bond authentication and distribution and the duties of the paying agent. The fiscal agent is a representative of the issuer. Eurobonds may be issued entirely outside the country in whose currency the bonds are denominated. The country in whose currency a bond is denominated can exercise control over the issue in a number of ways. One is by restricting access to its markets for other issues of uncooperative investment bankers. Also, since most currency transactions are settled in the domestic market for that currency, a government can effectively block bond issues through currency regulations.

7.3.3. Auctions

Auctions are used in a variety of ways in connection with debt instruments. Probably the most common use is in the issuance of securities. In the United States as well as in other countries, Treasury bills are typically issued through an auction procedure. Auctions have also been used in the repurchase of securities. Appendix 2-1 provides details concerning auctions.

8. Summary

The market for fixed income securities, which includes the markets for both private and governmental debt, is much larger than the market for equities. The two major segments of the market are the money market, which encompasses debt instruments with maturities of less than one year, and the capital market, which includes debt instruments with maturities of more than one year. Domestic markets are confined to a single country while the Eurocurrency market comprises all bank deposits and loans in any nondomestic currency.

Investors owning debt instruments face many types of risk. Some of the most important are: interest rate risk, the risk of capital losses due to increased interest rates; default risk, the risk that the issuer will not fulfill the terms of the bond contract; liquidity risk, the risk of being locked into an investment that cannot be readily sold; agency risk, the risk that the issuer will take actions that reduce the value of the investment; and sovereign risk, the risk that a governmental borrower will not fulfill its obligations. To help investors evaluate these risks a number of firms critically examine debt issues and issue an opinion in the form of a rating.

The most common types of money market instruments are: government issues such as Treasury bills; negotiable certificates of deposit (CD) issued by commercial banks evidencing time-deposits; commercial paper, a short-term unsecured promissory note issued by a corporation; repurchase agreements in which one party sells securities to a counterparty in exchange for an immediate payment with an agreement to repurchase the securities at a specified time and for a fixed price; reverse repurchase agreements in which there is an initial purchase with an agreement for a subsequent sale; call money, loans that are repayable at the request of either party; federal funds, deposits with the U.S. federal reserve system; and **bankers' acceptances**, a draft that orders a particular party to pay a specified amount at a specified time that has been acknowledged by the person required to made the payment and guaranteed by a bank.

Bonds are securities in which an issuer contractually agrees to make one or more payments to an investor. Bonds share similar features worldwide. The agreement between the bondholders and the issuer is called the indenture, which specifies the rights and obligations of the issuer and owners of the bonds, including the interest to be paid and the employment of various agents in the issuance of the securities. Some bonds can be exchanged or converted into other securities of the issuer or of another firm. Global bond markets, which are growing in importance, comprise two different types of issues. Foreign bonds include bonds issued in a country by nonresidents, in either the domestic currency or in a nondomestic currency. Eurobonds are trans-national bonds issues typically underwritten by an international investment banking syndicate.

Appendix 2-1. Auctions

Cassady (1967) defines an auction as a system of allocating property "based on price making by competition of buyers for the right to purchase." Auctions are useful in a variety of circumstances and often offer more speedy sales than alternates. Sometimes the purchaser has a more accurate assessment of the value of an item than the seller, especially for unique items such as antiques, art, and rare coins, books, stamps, and wine. The use of an auction may also solve agency problems by making it more difficult for the seller's agent to collude with the buyer.

For simplicity, Rasmusen (1989) categorizes auctions as either private-value or common-value. In private-value auctions each participant knows his/her own valuation with certainty, but may not know the valuations of other participants. Such a circumstance may result when individuals are buying for their own consumption or pleasure and not for resale. In its strict form, if the auction is private-value, individuals do not change their assessment of value given knowledge of others' proposed bids though they might change their bidding strategy. In contrast, for common-value auctions, each participant uses their own private information to estimate a true price. Knowledge of others assessments would be useful in assessing and validating one's private information. In this type of auction one's assessment is based on the asset's resale value rather than one's own internal assessment. Auctions for U.S. Treasury bills are common-value auctions since after the auction everyone agrees that the market price is the true value. Rasmusen (1989) further considers three common types of auctions:

English (also called first-price open-outcry) auction. After the beginning of the auction one participant initiates the bidding and subsequent bidders are then free to respond with higher bids. Participants are free to revise their bids at any time though there may be requirements that new bids exceed the current high bid by some minimum amount and only bids at certain values may be allowed. When no bidder wishes to make a higher bid, the item is sold to the high bidder at the bid price. Many agricultural commodities are sold at auction in the U.S. in this way.

First-price sealed bid. Each bidder submits a bid without knowing the bids of other participants. The highest bidder pays the amount of their bid and receives title to the object. Auctions of this type are common for Treasury bills. The Monetary Authority of Singapore (MAS) sends letters to financial institutions inviting bids for a fixed amount of Treasury bills. Each tender is for at least 250,000 SGD and must be submitted before a fixed time. The MAS ranks the bids by price from highest to lowest. The MAS goes down the bid schedule to identify the bid that exhausts the offer amount. All higher bids are filled first and the remaining supply is allocated pro rata to bids at the lowest successful price. The U.S. follows a similar procedure except that all purchasers pay the price of the lowest successful bidder. Both Singapore and the U.S. allow small orders that are not part of the biding process.

Dutch or descending auction. The auctioneer announces a bid that he continuously lowers until someone takes the object at that price. U.S. firms sometimes use a version of this procedure to repurchase their shares.[1] A firm will announce the number of shares to be repurchased (this is a USSEC regulation) and a price range. Individual stockholders will indicate the number of shares they are willing to sell at a given price. The firm will pay all shareholders the lowest price necessary to acquire the number of shares sought. All shareholders receive the same price (this is also an USSEC rule). Shareholders bidding the lowest successful price receive sell a pro rata number of shares based on the ratio of their quantity offered to the aggregate quantity offered at that price.

Questions

1. What are the most common types of risk faced by investors in bonds?
2. What are the differences between default risk and liquidity risk of debt investments?
3. What is the use of rating agencies to evaluate bond issues? What kind of firm-related factors do they consider while assessing the quality of debt issues?
4. What is the main difference between money markets and capital markets?

---

[1] Bagwell (1992) and Gay, Kale, and Noe (1996).

5. What kind of unsecured short-term debt instruments can be used by corporations to raise funds? Which firms can use these instruments?
6. What are the most common overnight investments used by U.S. banks?
7. Describe a bankers' acceptance and explain how it can be used to finance trade.
8. What are the characteristics of exchangeable and convertible bonds?
9. What is crisis at maturity and how can it be reduced?
10. What are the main hypotheses that have been advanced to explain the term structure?

References

Bagwell, Laurie Simon (1992), Dutch auction repurchases: An analysis of shareholder heterogeneity, Journal of Finance, 47, 71–105

Bilal, Gohar, 1999, Islamic finance: alternatives to the Western model, The Fletcher Forum of World Affairs 23, 145.

Cantor, Richard, and Frank Packer, 1996a, Determinants and impact of sovereign credit ratings, Federal Reserve Bank of New York Economic Policy Review, October, 37-53.

Cantor, Richard, and Frank Packer, 1996b, Multiple ratings and credit standards: differences of opinion in the credit rating industry, Federal Reserve Bank of New York, 12.

Cassady, Ralph, 1967, Auctions. Berkley, CA: University of California Press.

Cox, John C., Jonathan E. Ingersoll, Jr., and Stephen A. Ross, 1981, A reexamination of traditional hypotheses about the term structure of interest rates, Journal of Finance 36, 769-799.

Culbertson, J.W., 1957, The term structure of interest rates, Quarterly Journal of Economics 71, 485-517.

Diebold, Francis X., and Canlin Li, 2006, Forecasting the term structure of government bond yields, Journal of Econometrics 130, 337-364.

Fama, Eugene F., 1976, Forward rates as predictors of future spot rates, Journal of Financial Economics 3, 361-377.

Ferris, Andrew, F., 1991, The Financial Markets of Hong Kong. London: Routledge.

Fleming, Michael J., and Eli M. Remolona, 1996, Price formation and liquidity in the U.S. treasuries market: evidence from intraday patterns around announcements, Federal Reserve Bank of New York, no. 9633.

Froot, Kenneth A., 1989, New hope for the expectations hypothesis of the term structure of interest rates, Journal of Finance 44, 283-305.

Gay, Gerald D., Jayant R. Kale, and Thomas H. Noe, (Dutch) auction share repurchases, Economica 63, 249-57.

Gowland, D.H., 1990, International Bond Markets. London: Routledge.

Hickman, W. Braddock, 1958, Corporate Bond Quality and Investor Experience. New York: National Bureau of Economic Research

Karmin, Craig, and Gregory Zuckerman, 1998, U.S. firms step up volume of 'global' bond offerings, Wall Street Journal, September 2, p. C1.

McCulloch, J. Houston, 1975, An estimation of the liquidity premium, Journal of Political Economy 83, 95-119.

Meiselman, David, 1975, The Term Structure of Interest Rates. Englewood Cliffs. NJ: Prentice-Hall.

Melnik, Arie L., and Steven E. Plaut, 1991, The Short-term Eurocredit Market. Monograph Series in Finance and Economics. New York; New York University Salomon Center.

Modigliani, Franco, and Richard Sutch, 1966, Innovations in interest rate policy, American Economic Review 56, no. 2, 178-197.

Nelson, Charles, 1972, Estimation of term premiums from average yield differential in the term structure of interest rates, Econometrica 40, 277-287.

Packer, Frank, and Elizabeth Reynolds, 1997, The Samurai bond market, Current Issues in Economics and Finance, Federal Reserve Bank of New York 3.

Rasmusen, Eric, 1989, Games and Information: An Introduction to Game Theory. New York: Blackwell.

Repo and Securities Lending, 1977, Euromoney

Sarno, Lucio, Daniel L. Thornton, and Gioggio Valente, The empirical failure of the expectations hypothesis of the term structure of interest rates, Journal of Financial and Quantitative Analysis 42, 81-100.

Seligman, Joel, 1989, The Washington Public Power Supply System debacle, The Journal of Corporation Law 14, 889.

Sitzer, Howard D. , Cyrus Noe and James D. Perko, 1994, The Washington Public Power Supply System: then and now, Municipal Finance Journal 14, 59.

Takagi, Shinji, 1993, Japanese Capital Markets. Oxford: Blackwell.

Tatewaki, Kazuo, 1991, Banking and Finance in Japan. London: Routledge.

Urich, Thomas J., 1991, U.K., German and Japanese Government Bond Markets. Monograph Series in Finance and Economics. New York: New York University Salomon Center.

Yamamoto, Shigeru, 1993, The Japanese bond market, in Shinji Takagi (ed.), Japanese Capital Markets. Oxford, Blackwell, p. 217.

CHAPTER THREE

QUANTITATIVE ANALYSIS OF DEBT SECURITIES

Key Terms

Annuity—a series of payments of the same amount.

Current yield—a bond's annual coupon rate divided by the market price of the bond.

Duration—see Macaulay's duration.

Macaulay's duration—the measure of duration developed by Macaulay, which expresses the rate of change in the value of an asset in relation to the rate of change in interest rates.

Modified duration—Macaulay's duration divided by -(1 + y) where y is the yield-to-maturity or required return—this measure shows that for a given yield change there is an inverse relationship between modified duration and the percentage change in price.

Total realized compound yield—the expected annual yield of an investment over a stated horizon given an indicated reinvestment rate.

Yield-to-maturity—the discount rate that equates the future cash flows of a bond with the market price.

> IN THIS CHAPTER, we describe
> - procedures for calculating bond yields,
> - method for comparing one bond with another in making an investment decision, and
> - the importance, construction, and meaning of bond yield curves.
>
> Then, we define a measure of average bond life called duration and illustrate its uses.

1. Introduction

Over the last century a number of tools have been developed to analyze bonds. These tools are widely used by finance professionals and are standard parts of the C.F.A. curriculum and examinations. Moreover, individuals may find these tools useful in making their own investments. Hence, all students of finance should know and understand these tools. In this chapter we introduce three of the most widely used, namely, yield to maturity, total realized compound yield, and duration.

2. Time value of money

2.1. Introduction

The time value of money is one of the most important concepts in finance. Payments or cash flows are typically received over a period of time. The payments may vary from period to period or may represent an **annuity**, a series of payments that are the same in each period. According to the theory of finance, a set of cash flows that are received at given times can be converted into equivalent cash flows for any other set of times. This section explains how this is done.

Period n begins at time n-1 and ends at time n. In other words the first period (period 1) begins at time 0 and ends at time 1. Hence, any given number represents both the end of one period and the beginning of another. These payments are typically assumed to occur either uniformly over each period, which is called **continuous compounding,** or at the end of each period. In this book we will assume that all payments are at the end of each period.

Present value is the value of a series of cash flows at t = 0 given a set of interest rates. **Discounting** is the process of converting cash flows for t > 0 to an equivalent amount at time t = 0. **Future value** is the value of a series of cash flows at a stated period after period 1.

Present values and future values can be calculated with a financial calculator. Many calculators are programmed to calculate these values. However, in learning about how these values are calculated it is useful to calculate the values without using a computer program. Instead we will simply use the calculator to multiply, divide, add, and subtract.

Four interest-rate-factor or time-value-of-money tables are commonly provided. The construction of the tables depends on three variables: the number of periods, the interest rate per period, and the number of payments.

2.2. Present value of a single payment

The first table commonly provides factors for the present value of a single payment received (at the end of) n periods from t = 0. In other words, a discount factor is provided that, for an indicated interest rate, r, gives the equivalent at time t = 0 of a payment t+n periods in the future. The formula for the present value factor is $1/(1 + r)^n$. Table 3-1 provides an example of a present value table for a single payment.

Interest rates are typically expressed as a rate per year. If the market interest rate is 6% then 1 USD paid at the end of 4 years is worth 0.7921 USD at t = 0 (obtained by looking across the row for n=4 and down the column for r = 6%).

Suppose that instead of a year, the table is to be used for payments that occur multiple times each year such as quarterly or semiannually. Then it is necessary to divide the interest rate by the number of periods. In other words, if the market interest rate is 8% compounded semiannually, 1 USD payable at the end of four years is worth 0.7307 USD at the beginning of the first period. The appropriate factor is obtained by dividing the interest rate in half (because of the semiannual compounding) and then looking

Table 3-1. Present value factors for a single payment

Present value at time t = 0 of 1 unit payable at time t+n at interest rate r

(n is in column 1 and r is in the remaining rows)

n	4%	5%	6%	7%	8%
1	0.9615	0.9524	0.9434	0.9346	0.9259
2	0.9246	0.9070	0.8900	0.8734	0.8573
3	0.8890	0.8638	0.8396	0.8163	0.7938
4	0.8548	0.8227	0.7921	0.7629	0.7350
5	0.8219	0.7835	0.7473	0.7130	0.6806
6	0.7903	0.7462	0.7050	0.6663	0.6302
7	0.7599	0.7107	0.6651	0.6627	0.5835
8	0.7307	0.6768	0.6274	0.5820	0.5403
9	0.7026	0.6446	0.5919	0.5439	0.5002
10	0.6756	0.6139	0.5584	0.5083	0.4632

under the appropriate number of periods, which in this case is 8 (4 years X 2 compounding periods).

2.3. Future value of a single payment

Alternately, as shown in Table 3-2., a future value table comprising future value factors for a single payment n periods beyond t = 0 may be provided. For a given interest rate, r, these factors reflect the value at time t + n of one unit payable at time t = 0, which has the formula $(1 + r)^n$. The future value interest factor is the reciprocal of the present value interest factor. Selected future value interest factors are presented here: Again, if the interest rate is quoted as an annual rate and the actual compounding period is more frequent, the interest rate must be divided by n, the number of compounding periods, and the appropriate number of periods must be used when obtaining the future value factor from the table.

2.4. Present value of an annuity

The present value and future value tables are for use in evaluating single payments. Frequently, one needs to obtain the present value or future value

Table 3-2. Future value factors for a single payment
Future value at time t + n of 1 unit payable at time t at interest rate r.
(n is in column 1 and r is in the remaining columns)

	4%	5%	6%	7%	8%
1	1.0400	1.0500	1.0600	1.0700	1.0800
2	1.0816	1.1025	1.1236	1.1449	1.1664
3	1.1249	1.1576	1.1910	1.2250	1.2597
4	1.1699	1.2155	1.2625	1.3108	1.3605
5	1.2167	1.2763	1.3382	1.4026	1.4693
6	1.2653	1.3401	1.4185	1.5007	1.5869
7	1.3159	1.4071	1.5036	1.6058	1.7138
8	1.3686	1.4775	1.5938	1.7182	1.8509
9	1.4233	1.5513	1.6895	1.8385	1.9990
10	1.4802	1.6289	1.7908	1.9672	2.1589

of an annuity. It is possible to use the tables that we have already examined. However, annuities are so common that it is typical to adjust these tables to deal with them. The formula for the present value annuity factor is $(1 - (1/(1 + r)^n)/r$. Note that the present value annuity factors can be constructed from the present value factors. For period 1 the present value annuity factor and the present value factor are the same. For period 2, the present value annuity factor is the sum of the present value factor for periods 1 and 2. For period 3, the present value annuity factor is the sum of the present value factors for period 1, 2 and 3. Table 3-3 shows present value annuity factors.

If the market interest rate is 6%, the present value at time t of 1USD paid at the end of periods 1-4 is 3.4651 USDs (obtained by looking across row 4 and down the column for r + 6%). If semiannual compounding is used, the annual interest rate must be divided by 2 and the number of periods must be multiplied by 2. Note that the values in row 1 of Table 3-3 and Table 3-3 are the same.

2.5. Future value of an annuity

While the table for the future value of single payments can be used to evaluate an annuity, a separate table such as Table 3-4 is typically provided. The formula for future value annuity factors is $((1 + r)^n - 1)/r$.

Table 3-3. Present value factors for an annuity

Present value annuity factors. Each factor represents the present value of 1 unit payable at the end of each of n periods at the interest rate r.
(n is in column 1 and r is in the remaining columns)

	4%	5%	6%	7%	8%
1	0.9615	0.9524	0.9494	0.9346	0.9529
2	1.8861	1.8594	1.8334	1.8080	1.7833
3	2.7751	2.7323	2.6730	2.6243	2.5771
4	3.6299	3.5460	3.4651	3.3872	3.3121
5	4.4518	4.3295	4.2124	4.1002	3.9927
6	5.2421	5.0757	4.9173	4.7665	4.6229
7	6.0021	5.7864	5.5824	5.3893	5.2064
8	6.7327	6.4632	6.2098	5.9713	5.7466
9	7.4353	7.1078	6.8017	6.5152	6.2469
10	8.1109	7.7217	7.3601	7.0236	6.7101

The table for future value annuity factors can also be constructed from the table for future value factors, but the procedure is somewhat different than for the present value case. For the future value annuity table, the entries for period 1 are all 1.0000, regardless of the interest rate. This is because we are receiving the first payment at the end of the first period and there is no compounding.

Consider the entry for a 4% interest rate for n = 3. Examining the future value table for periods 1-3 we see: period 1, 1.0400; period 2, 1.0816; and period 3, 1.1249. The entry for period 3 in the future value annuity table is the sum of the first two entries in the future value table (1.0400 + 1.0816 = 2.1216) plus 1, which gives 3.1216. In each case, the entries in the future value annuity table for period n is 1 plus the sum of the entries in future value table for period 1 through period n-1.

If the compounding period is more frequent than annually, then the yearly interest rate must be divided by the number of periods and the yearly number of periods must be multiplied by the number of periods in each year (i.e., 2 for semiannual, 4 for quarterly, and 12 for monthly).

Table 3-4. Future value factors for an annuity

Future value annuity factors. Each factor represents the future value of 1 unit payable at the end of each of n periods at the interest rate r.
(n is in column 1 and r is in row 1)

	4%	5%	6%	7%	8%
1	1.0000	1.0000	1.0000	1.0000	1.0000
2	2.0400	2.0500	2.0600	2.0700	2.0800
3	3.1216	3.1525	3.1836	3.2149	3.2464
4	4.2465	4.3101	4.3746	44399	4.5061
5	5.4163	5.5256	5.6371	5.7507	5.8686
6	6.6330	6.8019	6.9753	7.1533	7.3359
7	7.8983	8.1420	8.3938	8.6540	8.9228
8	9.2142	9.5491	9.8975	10.260	10.637
9	10.583	11.027	11.491	11.978	12.488
10	12.006	12.578	13.181	13.816	14.487

Beyond row 1, the entries in the future value annuity table can be constructed from the future value table. To see this consider the follow revised version of Table 3-2 in which all of the values have been moved forward one period and the value of 1.0000 has been added as row 1:

Table 3-5. Future value factors for a single payment (revised)

Future value at time t + n of 1 unit payable at time t at interest rate r.
(n is in column 1 and r is in the remaining columns)

	4%	5%	6%	7%	8%
1	1.0000	1.0000	1.0000	1.0000	1.0000
2	1.0400	1.0500	1.0600	1.0700	1.0800
3	1.0816	1.1025	1.1236	1.1449	1.1664
4	1.1249	1.1576	1.1910	1.2250	1.2597
5	1.1699	1.2155	1.2625	1.3108	1.3605
6	1.2167	1.2763	1.3382	1.4026	1.4693
7	1.2653	1.3401	1.4185	1.5007	1.5869
8	1.3159	1.4071	1.5036	1.6058	1.7138
9	1.3686	1.4775	1.5938	1.7182	1.8509
10	1.4233	1.5513	1.6895	1.8385	1.9990
	1.4802	1.6289	1.7908	1.9672	2.1589

Now it is clear that each value for a given row and column in Table 3-4 can be obtained by summing all of the values in the same column of Table 3-5 from row 1 with the values for all the other rows up to and including the same row.

3. Current yield and yield-to-maturity

3.1. Current yield

Unlike common stocks, most bonds promise a fixed series of future cash flows. It is common practice to calculate measures that summarize this cash flow stream. The **current yield** is the bond's annual coupon rate divided by the market price of the bond.

3.2. Calculating yield-to-maturity

The market price of the bond (P) is:

$$P = C/(1 + y)^1 + C/(1 + y)^2 + C/(1 + y)^3 + \ldots + C/(1 + y)^n + F/(1 + y)^n$$

where

C = the periodic coupon payment on the bond,

F = the payment on the bond at maturity, and

y = the bond's yield to maturity.

If C is paid semiannually, y is one half of the annual yield-to-maturity. If P, C and F are known, then the bond's yield-to-maturity can be calculated. The yield-to-maturity cannot be found analytically, but only by trial and error. The trial and error process can be facilitated by recognizing that if market interest rates equal the coupon rate of a given bond the market price of the bond will be 100, which means the price is 100% of face value.

Let's calculate the yield-to-maturity for a bond with a coupon rate of 6% paid semi-annually, two years until maturity, a maturity value of 1,000 USD and a current market price of 982 USD. If market interest rate is 6% the market value of the bond would be 100 (i.e., 100% of face value). Moreover, since bond prices fall when interest rates rise and the market value of the bond is less than 1,000 USD, we know that the yield-to-maturity is higher than 6%. Finding yield-to-maturity is a trial and error process. Let us begin by calculating the market value of the bond if market interest rates were 8%, which is:

$$30 (0.9615 + 0.9246 + 0.8890 + 0.8548) + (0.8548 \times 1030) = 963.70$$

Note that following custom we discount both the coupon payments and the final payment at maturity using the semiannual rate. Given our result of 963.70, which is less than 982, we know that the yield-to-maturity is between 6% and 8%. We can obtain a more exact yield-to-maturity by testing additional values or by using a calculator. We can obtain an approximation using linear interpolation, which we illustrate next.

We know that 6% and 8% discount rates produce market values of 1,000 and 963.70, respectively. We wish to know the yield-to-maturity associated with a market price of 982. Define the following:

$$A = 1,000 - 982 = 18,$$

$$B = 1,000 - 963.70 = 36.3,$$

$$C = 6\% - ?\%, \text{ and}$$

$$D = 6\% - 8\% = -2\%$$

Then, $A/B = C/D$ so that

$$(A/B)D = C.$$

Substituting values gives

$$(-2\%)(18/36.3) = 6\% - ?\%.$$

Rearranging terms and simplifying gives

$$?\% = 6.99.$$

Hence, the estimated yield-to-maturity is 6.99%.

Naturally, today investors use calculators or computers to solve yield-to-maturity problems. But the calculators and computers are simply solving net present value problems over and over until they find a solution that is satisfactorily close to the yield to maturity. There is no analytical way to find an exact solution. If you would like to use Excel, then enter the follow into the Excel spreadsheet:

	A	B
1	Current price of the bond	-982
2	Coupon payment	30
3	Coupon payment	30
4	Coupon payment	30
5	Coupon payment plus return of principal	1030
6		

Then place the cursor in row 6 of column B and enter =IRR(B1:B5)*2 into the f_x location above the A heading. The "*2" is needed to convert the semiannual rate into an annual rate. Hitting return will return the yield to maturity, which in this case is 0.0698.

4. Total realized compound yield

As we have already noted, the yield-to-maturity is the internal rate of return for a bond. It is well known in capital budgeting that the internal rate of return has a number of limitations, especially in comparisons of one investment with another. These limitations also apply to comparisons of one bond with another. The two most important limitations in bond comparisons are the reinvestment rate problem and the horizon problem.

Suppose that an investor wants to compare the relative merits of two bonds with the same maturity but different coupon rates, over a stated horizon, say three years. Suppose further that each bond has an identical yield-to-maturity. On the basis of yield-to-maturity the two bonds are equally attractive. The problem with this conclusion is that the reinvestment rate of the cash flows may differ from the yield-to-maturity. If these cash flows can be reinvested at a rate higher than the yield-to-maturity then the bond with the higher coupons is more attractive since these intermediate cash flows can be invested more favorably. If the comparison were made using yield-to-maturity this feature of the two investments would be entirely missed.

A related problem in making comparison based on yield-to-maturity is called the horizon problem. In this case consider two bonds with the same coupon rate and yield-to-maturity, but with differing maturates. Here again the yield-to-maturity fails to capture the possibility that the proceeds from the bond with the earlier maturity may be invested at either a higher or lower rate than the yield-to-maturity. If expected market interest rates are higher (lower) than the yield-to-maturity the shortest (longest) lived bond is probably the best alternative.

In comparing two bonds the appropriate approach is to calculate the expected future value of each investment over the investor's investment horizon using a projected reinvestment rate. This future value can then be annualized over the investment horizon to produce the total realized compound yield. If the investment horizon is n years, then the **total realized compound yield** is (future value/initial value)^n - 1. If the compounding period is semiannual, n is the number of semiannual periods and the result must be multiplied by 2 to obtain an annual rate. Note that the investor's investment horizon can be longer or shorter than the maturity of any given investment. If a bond is used that has a shorter maturity than the investor's investment horizon, then the future value must include the return from investing the proceeds of the bond at maturity along with the return from investing the intermediate cash flows. If a bond with a longer maturity than the investment horizon is used then the market value of the bond at the end of the investment horizon must be calculated.

Next, we calculate total realized compound yield when the investment horizon is the same as the bond maturity and when it is longer.

1. Calculate the total realized compound yield given the following information:

Bond maturity:	3 years
Bond coupon rate (semiannual payments):	6%
Bond face value:	1,000
Bond price (% of face value):	79
Reinvestment rate:	8%
Investment horizon:	3 years

Step 1: Calculate the future value

(6.6330 X 30) + 1,000 = 1198.99

Step 2: Calculate the total realized compound yield

$[(1198.99/790)^{1/6} - 1] \times 2 = 0.072 \times 2 = 0.1440$ or 14.4%

2. Next, calculate the total realized compound yield for the same bond, but now assuming an investment horizon of 5 years:

Step 1: Calculate the future value

$((6.6330 \times 30) + 1{,}000) \times 1.1699 = 1402.69$

Step 2: Calculate the total realized compound yield

$[(1402.69/790)^{1/10} - 1] \times 2 = 0.0591 \times 2 = 0.1182$ or 11.825%

5. Duration

5.1. How duration works

We have seen that the term structure of interest rates can be upward sloping or downward sloping depending on expectations for future spot interest rates. Suppose that we wish to know how a uniform change in the term structure affects the price of a bond. Consider a bond that pays interest semiannually for n years, that has a coupon payment of C and a maturity value of F. Let y be the required yield. If interest rates are expressed on a per year basis and the bond has semiannual payments, y is one-half the annual rate and the periods are semiannual periods. If the bond payments are on an annual basis, y is the annual interest rate and the periods are annual periods. As we saw above, if y is the required yield the market price of the bond (P) must be:

$$P = C/(1+y)^1 + C/(1+y)^2 + C/(1+y)^3 + \ldots + C/(1+y)^n + M/(1+y)^n$$

To determine the change in price for a small change in y, we take the first derivative and rearrange terms to obtain

$$dP/dy = -(1/(1+y))[(c/(1+y)^1) + (2c/(1+y)^2) + \ldots$$
$$+ (nC/(1+y)^n) + (nM/(1+y)^n)]$$

Multiplying both sides by 1/P gives

$$dP/dy\,(1/P) = -(1/(1+y))[(c/(1+y)^1) + (2c/(1+y)^2) + \ldots$$
$$+ (nC/(1+y)^n) + (nM/(1+y)^n)](1/P) \qquad 3.1$$

The quantity in brackets multiplied by (1/P) is known as **Macaulay's duration**. From equation 3.1 we can see that Macaulay's duration is

$$-dP/dy\,(1/P)\,(1+y)$$

Dividing Macaulay's duration by $(1+y)$ gives a measure known as **modified duration**. Modified duration is the percentage change in a bond's price for a 100 basis points change in yield. Both duration measures discussed so far assume that a change in interest rates does not affect the bond cash flows. Call options and other options associated with a bond might make this assumption unreasonable. Effective duration is a duration measure that is designed to address this issue. Other duration measures may address other shortcomings of the simple duration measures such as the assumption of a uniform shift in the yield curve.

Duration provides a summary measure that is useful in comparing individual bond issues and bond portfolios. Broadly speaking, duration can be viewed as the average life of a bond. Macaulay's duration deals with a uniform shift in the yield curve. For small movements in the yield curve bonds with the same duration will experience the same change in price. This characteristic gives duration a role in investment management and in the management of financial institutions. Banks, insurance companies and other financial institutions have both assets and liabilities whose values fluctuate with changing interest rates. It may be desirable to attempt to see that interest rate induced changes in liabilities are matched by comparable interest rate induced change in the value of assets. Otherwise, if changes in interest rates cause the value of liabilities to increase while the value of assets does not increase by a corresponding amount (or even decreases) the firm may face insolvency or bankruptcy.

A portfolio or balance sheet whose overall position is not affected by interest rate changes is called **immunized**. Some financial institutions may find it more difficult to immunize their asset/liability positions by the judicious choice of investments. This is especially true if the assets or liabilities that need to be immunized have particularly short or long horizons. Banks have substantial liabilities in the form of demand deposits most of which have a duration of zero. Assets with similarly short maturities include federal funds.

There are some regularities concerning duration that it is worthwhile to know:
- The duration of a portfolio is the weighted average of the durations of the individual bonds in the portfolio where the weights are the proportion of current market value invested in each bond,
- Except for certain deep-discount bonds, holding other factors constant, the duration of a bond increases with its maturity,
- Holding other factors constant, the duration of a bond decreases with an increase in its interest rate,
- The duration of a perpetual annuity is $(1 + y)/y$, where y is the yield.
- If T is the number of payments, the duration of an annuity is
$$[(1 + y)/y] - [T/((1 + y)^T - 1)],$$
- The duration of a zero coupon bond is equal to the maturity of the bond.

5.2. Calculating duration

Assume that we have a bond with an 8% coupon rate that pays interest semi-annually and has 2 years to maturity. Market interest rates are 10%. The following shows how the duration of this bond is calculated.

Periods in years	Cash flow	Present value at 5%	Weight	Weight X periods
0.5	40	38.10	0.0395	0.0197
1.0	40	36.28	0.0376	0.0376
1.5	40	34.55	0.0358	0.0537
2.0	1040	855.61	0.8871	1.7741
		964.54	1.0000	
			Duration:	1.8851

The duration of this bond is 1.8851 years.

5.3. How interest rate changes affect duration

Suppose that an investor can invest in three zero-coupon bonds—one with a one-year maturity, one with a 1.5 year maturity, and one with a two year maturity. We know that the duration of each of these bonds equals its maturity. Assume that the investor has a 1.5 year horizon. If market interest rates are 5% and the 1.5 year bond has a face value of 1,000, its current market value is $1,000/1.05^{1.5} = 929.43$. Hence, by investing 929.43 in the 1.5 year bond the investor can receive 1,000 in 1.5 years without interest rate risk. Suppose instead that the investor invests 929.43/2 each in the one-year and two year bonds. The duration of this two-bond portfolio is:

Periods in years	Current market value at 5%	Weight	Weight X periods
1.0	464.715	0.5	0.5
2.0	464.715	0.5	1.0
	929.430	1.0	
		Duration:	1.5

Suppose interest rates increase by 10 basis points. The one year bond will be worth $(464.715 \times 1.05)1.05^{0.5} = 500$. And the 2 year bond will be worth $(464.715 \times 1.05^2)/1.051^{0.5} = 500$. Hence, the value of the two-bond portfolio has not changed. The increase in value of investing the 1,000 received at the end of the first year has offset the decline in the value of the two-year bond. Given our assumptions that shifts in the yield curve are uniform, any bond or portfolio with the same duration will be equally suitable to protect against interest rate changes over the duration horizon. In reality there might not be a 1.5 year bond available so that the two-bond portfolio would be the only option.

5.4. How duration is used in bank asset liability management

Suppose that a bank has 1,000 USD of assets with a duration of 7 years and liabilities of 1,000 USD with a duration of 7 years. Current interest rates are 10%. How much equity does a bank need to be able to absorb a 1% change in interest rates and still have equity of 50 USD?

We know that

$$\Delta P = -(1/(1 + y)) \text{ Macaulay duration} \times \Delta y$$

Therefore, the change in value of the liability portfolio is $1000[(1/(1.1)) \times 0.01] = -9.09$ USD and the decline in value of the asset portfolio is

1000[(7/(1.1)) X 0.01] = -63.64 USD. The net change in shareholders' equity is -63.64 USD - (-9.09 USD) or -54.55 USD. Hence, to insure that stockholders' equity is at least 50 USD if interest rates increase 1%, the bank must have initial equity of 50 USD + 54.55 USD = 104.55 USD.

6. Summary

There are a variety of short term debt instruments that mature in less than a year and often in only a few days. These include Treasury bills, bankers' acceptances, Federal funds, commercial paper, call money loans and negotiable certificates of deposit. Rather than having a stated interest rate many money market instruments are sold at a discount from face value. The money markets are used by governments to bridge short term gaps between expenditures and tax receipts and by companies as an alternative to bank loans. Both governments and firms use money market instruments to invest funds not needed immediately.

Most debt securities with longer maturities make one or more fixed payments prior to maturity. The expected payments are typically stated as a coupon rate that is a percentage of the bond's face value. Interest rates are usually stated on an annual basis even if the payments are made quarterly or semi-annually. Investors are often interested in determining their return on holding debt securities. The current yield is the coupon rate divided by the market price of the bond. The yield-to-maturity is the rate of return that equates the fixed payment series to the bond's market price. The yield-to-maturity cannot be calculated analytically, but must be determined through trial and error or by using a computer or calculator.

Yield-to-maturity is the same as internal rate of return. It is well known that there are problems in using the internal rate of return to compare investments. A particularly important problem in comparing bonds is that the reinvestment rate might differ from the yield-to-maturity. To overcome these problems, bonds can be compared using total realized compound yield.

Macaulay's duration measures the average life of a bond taking both interest payments and principal repayment into account. If a bond promises only one future payment at the maturity of the bond, the duration of the bond is the same as its maturity. But if a bond makes a number of payments before making the final payment at maturity, the duration of the bond is less than the maturity of the bond. When interest rates change, portfolios with the same duration have the same change in value. Hence, duration can be a useful tool in managing financial assets. Suppose that a financial institution is borrowing money in order to make investments. Both the assets and liabilities of the institution are subject to interest rate risk. If the liabilities have more risk than the assets the firm runs the risk that an increase in interest rates will result in financial ruin. The financial institution can limit or eliminate this risk by its choice of the duration of the asset and liability portfolios. If each portfolio has the same duration the combined asset/liability portfolio is protected or immunized from changes in value due to interest rate changes

Questions

1. What limitations make yield-to-maturity inappropriate for comparing the relative merits of investing in two bonds.
2. When comparing two bonds in making an investment decision, what measure would be more useful than yield-to-maturity?
3. Why is duration a more appropriate indicator of interest rate risk than maturity?
4. How is a bond's coupon rate related to its duration?
5. What is the definition of yield-to-maturity?
6. Why are financial institutions concerned with the durations of their assets and liabilities?

References

Hicks, J., 1939, Value and Capital. London: Oxford University Press.

Macaulay, Frederick, 1938, Some Theoretical Problems Suggested by the Movement of Interest Rates, Bond Yields, and Stock Prices in the U.S. Since 1956. New York: National Bureau of Economic Research.

Bierwag, G.O., G. G. Kaufman, and A Toevs, 1983, Duration: Its development and use in bond portfolio management, Financial Analysts Journal 39 (Jul - Aug), 15-35.

CHAPTER FOUR

GLOBAL CURRENCY MARKETS (FOREIGN EXCHANGE)

Key Terms

American terms—a currency quotation for which the unit of account, i.e., the currency measured in 1 unit, is not the USD.

Big figure—the number that must be added to the quoted shorthand price to complete the quote.

Big number—see big figure.

Countertrade—the exchange of goods for goods in international trade so that no money exchanges hands between the buyer and seller.

Cross-rate—an exchange rate between two currencies, neither of which is the USD.

Currency swap—the exchange of two currencies at a stated exchange rate with an agreement to reverse the transaction at a stated future date.

Direct quote—the price of one unit of a nondomestic currency in terms of the domestic currency.

Discount—if the exchange rate for future delivery is different from the current spot rate, the currency that is worth less in the future.

European terms—a currency quotation for which the USD is the unit of account so that the quote is so many units of currency per 1 USD.

Exotic currency—a currency that is not one of the major currencies.

Foreign exchange—currencies.

Foreign exchange swaps—the standard type of forward trade in the interbank market in which in a single agreement two currencies are exchanged now with a subsequent exchange in the reverse direction at an agreed future date.

Forward—foreign exchange transactions for settlement beyond the normal settlement date.

Forward points—same as swap points.

Hard currency—a currency that is freely and readily tradable.

Indirect quotation—the price of one unit of a domestic currency in terms of a nondomestic currency.

Outright forward—a forward contract that requires a single exchange of two currencies at a future date beyond the normal settlement date.

Pip—the last unit of measurement in a foreign exchange quotation.

Point—see pip.

Premium (in forex)—if the exchange rate for future delivery is different from the current spot rate, the currency that is worth more in the future.

Reciprocal quotation—a quotation that is the reciprocal of the quotation normally used.

Spot—the market for immediate delivery according to established settlement times.

Swap points—the bid and ask prices in a swap and the values used to determine the bids and asks for outright forwards.

> IN THIS CHAPTER, we discuss currencies (foreign exchange). Specifically, we:
> - Provide an overview of trading in foreign exchange,
> - Explain how foreign exchange is traded and quoted for immediate delivery (the spot market), and
> - Describe the currency transactions that involve exchanges beyond the standard settlement date (forward markets).

1. Introduction

The foreign exchange (forex) market, which is the market for currencies, is enormous with an average daily turnover of over 5 trillion USD and more than 87% of the trading involves just one currency, the USD, on one side.[1] There are large markets for both immediate delivery and future delivery. More than 50% of foreign exchange transactions are between parties in different countries, and more than 60% are interbank transactions. Trade sizes of 10 million USD or more are typical. Interbank trading, which is the focus of this chapter, provides enormous liquidity. The interbank wholesale market facilitates the trading of forex by others. Central banks often trade forex to influence the price of a domestic currency relative to the price of other currencies. Brokers are also involved in trading forex. The retail market mostly involves transactions between banks and the banks' nonblank customers and businesses involved in international trade or with facilities in more than one country that need buy and sell currencies in the forex market. Speculators with a view about the relative values of currencies also trade. Speculators seek to profit by predicting changes in the relative values of currencies and as much as 90% of daily trading volume may be motivated by speculation. Individuals may have investments in more than one country or need foreign exchange for travel. Smaller banks, companies needing foreign exchange, and both wealthy and small individuals also access the forex market for both speculation and operating needs.

2. Foreign exchange markets

2.1. Overview

There are two basic types of foreign exchange trades—spot and forward. The **spot** market is the market for immediate delivery according to established settlement times. Agreements for trades beyond the normal settlement times are **forward** transactions. There are two types of

---

[1] In this book we use the International Standards Organization (ISO) three digit codes for currencies. These codes are generally used for official purposes and by businesses rather than the outdated currency signs such as the $. http://en.wikipedia.org/wiki/ISO_4217

forwards—**foreign exchange swaps** and **outright forwards**. Only the forex swaps are traded in the interbank market and this type of forward transaction constitutes the bulk of forward transactions. In a forex swap two currencies are exchanged now with a subsequent exchange in the reverse direction at an agreed date. According to the Bank for International Settlements (2013),[1] slightly less than 40 percent of foreign exchange transactions are in the spot market and more than 40% are forex swaps.[2] **Outright forwards** call for the exchange of currencies at a future date and are constructed from forex swaps and spot trades and sold by brokers and banks to end users.

2.2. Organization of the foreign exchange market

The foreign exchange market is an over-the-counter market without a central location. Most foreign exchange trading is among several hundred large banks in countries all over the world. These banks trade directly with each other using telephones and electronic communications systems. Prior to trading with each other, the banks enter into an agreement such as the International Foreign Exchange Master Agreement.[3] This agreement spells out the relationship between the parties including details concerning delivery and netting. Since foreign exchange trading gives rise to claims against the bank's trading partners that may amount to as much as the aggregate value of the trades consummated, each bank also establishes a credit limit for each of the other banks with which it will deal in the interbank market. This limit is based on the credit worthiness of the customer bank and the size of the bank extending the credit.

Several characteristics of the direct interbank market may affect the desirability of trading there. Quotes in the interbank market are always two-sided, comprising both a bid and an ask or offer. Hence, a bank that wants to establish a long position may find itself selling rather than buying. Also, the identity of the counterparty is known. This creates an obligation for

---

[1] http://www.bis.org/publ/rpfx13fx.pdf

[2] A number of authors provide useful introductions to the forex market (Bishop 1992; Carew and Slatyer 1994; Luca 1995; Manuell 1986; and Walmsley 1992).

[3] http://www.newyorkfed.org/fmlg/ifemagui.pdf

reciprocity. Banks that call and initiate trades expect to be called when their trading partners have trades to initiate. Ordinarily, this would be beneficial, but in some cases, a bank might wish to trade without creating reciprocity expectations. If the currency is not one regularly dealt in, it may be difficult for the bank to meet the reciprocity expectations of its counterparties.

Because of the disadvantages of direct dealing, banks also commonly use foreign exchange brokers. Large speculators can also deal either with banks or brokers. These brokers do not take positions themselves, but, instead, intermediate the trading of others. Foreign exchange brokers such as Tullet Prebon have offices in major cities throughout the world.[1] Foreign exchange brokers are able to provide quick and broad coverage of the market, which enhances both the trader's feel for the market and the trader's ability to trade with multiple counterparties simultaneously. Trading through brokers is anonymous, which can prevent the identity of the bank initiating a trade from influencing the direction of the market and also avoids creating reciprocity expectations. Also, banks can offer one-sided quotes through brokers. This might provide an opportunity to improve on the best currently available market price on one side of the market without facing the possibility that the bank will have to trade on the other side.

Retail customers can also purchase foreign exchange through dealers such as FINEX, a currency dealer with inventories of more than 100 major and exotic currencies.[2]

Several ECNs provide a platform on which institutional clients can trade foreign exchange. Hotspot is an ECN serving the institutional market. Over sixty currency pairs can be traded with complete anonymity.[3] BAXTER-FX operates platforms that allow clients to connect to multiple ECNs.[4] Thomson Reuters Matching is an anonymous electronic matching platform

---

[1] http://www.tullettprebon.com/
[2] Forex Capital Markets (FXCM) is an online foreign exchange broker providing direct market access to manor banks rather than acting as a dealer. FXCM servers both small and large retail clients and institutions. http://www.finexforex.ca/?lang=en
[3] http://www.hotspotfx.com/
[4] http://www.baxter-fx.com/

for forex. We describe three of its platforms. Forward Matching, with more than 800 subscriber banks, offers real-time executable prices for 85 currency pairs with tenors (durations) from overnight to one year. Spot Matching, with over 1,100 subscriber banks, is the leading anonymous electronic trade matching system for the interbank spot market; trading is available in 80 currency pairs. Matching for Prime Brokerage allows prime broker clients to trade with anonymous direct market access.[1]

Thomson Reuters's major competitor is Electronic Brokering Services.[2] FXall has a trading platform on which more than 80 market makers offer streaming prices for over 500 currency pairs to more than 1,300 institutional clients.[3] Intergral is a regulated trading platform for the trading of non-deliverable forwards through either a limit order book or request for quotes.[4] Currenex offers a trading platform that provides executable streaming prices for both spot and forward forex.[5] Clients can place standard and many sophisticated types of orders including hidden and iceberg orders and orders with different expiry conditions.

2.3. Avoiding confusion

All foreign exchange transactions involve two currencies. While this may seem straight forward, in reality, it can be quite confusing. Hopefully, recognizing several potential sources of confusion will help avoid them. When dealing with, say, wheat, we might speak of buying or selling wheat for USD. It would be very unusual to speak of buying and selling USD for wheat. But in the foreign exchange market one might just as easily speak about buying or selling CHF for USD or buying and selling USD for CHF. What makes this potentially confusing is that buying CHF using USD is exactly the same as selling USD for CHF. Further, neither currency might be a domestic currency for the trader.

---

[1] http://thomsonreuters.com/matching/
[2] http://en.wikipedia.org/wiki/Electronic_Broking_Services
[3] http://www.fxall.com/about
[4] http://www.integral.com/about_integral/
[5] http://www.currenex.com/trading_services_esp.html; http://en.wikipedia.org/wiki/Currenex

Also, for every trade there is both a buyer and a seller. In order to understand the motivation and actions of the participants in the foreign exchange market it is important to keep in mind which firms are doing the buying and selling. The two parties to most trades are the market maker and the non-market maker. The market maker sells at the ask and buys at the bid while the non-market maker sells at the bid and buys at the ask. Examples can be constructed from either point of view.

Another source of confusion is the use of the terms swap and forward. As already defined, a forward is a trade with a settlement date beyond the standard spot settlement date and a swap combines a spot and forward trade in a single transaction. In this chapter the term swap always refers to a foreign exchange swap, which is the only type of forward trading done in the interbank foreign exchange market. In contrast, a **currency swap** involves the exchange of long-dated borrowing denominated in different currencies. Another potential source of confusion is that the term forward may be used to mean either a foreign exchange swap or an outright forward, which is a combination of a swap and a spot trade. We explain outright forwards more fully later. In this text we are careful to distinguish forward swaps and outright forwards.

Some authors use the terms direct and indirect to describe quotations. We find this terminology potentially confusing and therefore do not use it.

There is some potential confusion over the use of the term direct quotation. One author defines a direct quotation as "representing the value measured by number of dollars per unit."[1] Using this definition, the direct quotation for 1 AUD would be, say, 0.9750 USD. Alternately, others indicate that a direct quote is an exchange rate expressed in terms of the domestic currency, which would give Australia, USD1/AUD1.0256).[2] Clearly, these definitions are not the same. The first definition takes the viewpoint of a particular country, in this case the U.S., and ignores other countries. But a definition that changes depending on where one is can be very confusing. In this book we take a global perspective. Hence, to avoid confusion, we do not use the terms direct and indirect quotation. But if one

---

[1] Madura (1995, p. 706).
[2] Allan, Elstone, Lock, and Valentine, 1990, p. 217.

must we suggest that a **direct quote** expresses the price of one unit of a nondomestic currency in terms of the domestic currency. And an **indirect quote** expresses the price of one unit of a domestic currency in terms of a nondomestic currency. Thus, a quotation of AUD1/0.9750USD would be a direct quotation in the U.S. but an indirect quotation in Australia. And a quotation of USD1/AUD1.0256 is indirect in the U.S. and direct in Australia.

3. Dealing in foreign exchange markets

3.1. Spot market

3.1.1. Quoting American and European terms (ignoring spreads)

There are two ways of quoting foreign exchange—**American terms** and **European terms**. American terms is the same way that all prices are quoted in the U.S., the USD price of one unit of the item. In other words, the price of a loaf of bread in the U.S. is, say, 1.90 USD. Using this same approach, the price of one JPY is 0.0120 USD and the price of one CHF is 0.91 USD.[1]

For the European method the unit of trade is one USD. The quotation then indicates the number of units of the local currency that have the same value as one USD. Prices in European terms are the reciprocal of the price in American terms. The European method is used throughout the world for almost all currencies. Exceptions include the British pound, the Irish punt, the Australian and New Zealand dollars, and the South African rand. The use of American quotes for these currencies is a holdover from the days when the GBP was not a decimal currency. A **reciprocal quotation** is a quotation that is the reciprocal of the quotation normally used. In other words, for the GBP a reciprocal quotation would be in European terms.

---

[1] For spot quotes for a wide range of currencies see:
http://quotes.reuters.com/
http://www.oanda.com/converter/classic or
http://www.citibank.com/us/investments/market/.

3.1.2. Two-sided spot quotes using American and European terms

Of course, dealers do not typically quote one price. Instead, they quote a price at which they are willing to sell, the ask, and a price and which they are willing to buy, the bid. Naturally, the bid is lower than the ask. If one bank called another and asked for a CHF quote, the response might be: 1.6557/1.6568 or 1.6557/68 or even 57/68. This quotation is a USD/CHF exchange rate. All major currencies except the JPY are quoted to four decimal places. The quotation of 57/68 omits the **big figure** or the **big number**, which is the number that must be added to the quoted shorthand price to complete the quote. This shorthand convention is used to save time because the markets are very active. Since everyone is supposed to know where the market is trading and what the big figure is, there is no need to announce it. For currencies quoted in four decimal places, 0.0001 is called either a **pip** or a **point**. For the JYP a pip is 0.01.

Consider further the quotation of USD/CHF 1.6557/68. The first amount can be viewed as the bid and the second as the ask. But bid and ask for what? The answer is that the bid indicates how many CHF will be paid for one USD and the ask indicates how many CHF it will take to buy one USD. Hence, if a dealer could buy at the bid and sell at the ask, there would be a gain of 1.6568 - 1.6557 = 0.0011 CHF. For the AUD the quotation might be AUD/USD 0.6963/70. In this case the dealer is offering to buy one AUD for 0.6963 USD or sell one AUD for 0.6070 USD. For each AUD traded at the bid and ask, the dealer will have a gain of 0.6070 - 0.6963 = 0.0007 USD.

Note that we have chosen to indicate the currency that is expressed as a unit on the left hand side of the "/." This is standard practice in forex markets, but not in economics texts.

Banks use services provided by firms such as Telerate, Knight Ridder, and Reuters to transmit indicative quotes. Some banks might use all of these while others use none, relying instead on telephone calls from their customers.

Some banks make markets in many currencies while others specialize in only one or a small number of currencies. The three major currencies traded in foreign exchange markets after the USD are (in order by size) the EUR, JPY, and GBP. Goodhart and Demos (1991) ranked international financial centers based on the number of Reuters entries entered by each center. This measure of relative size is biased in that not all market makers use Reuters (some use competing services and some use dealers) and the relative penetration of Reuters differs by geographic area. Nevertheless, the use of Reuters entries as a basis for broad rankings is probably acceptable.

One way of identifying financial centers that are truly international is by whether dealers located in that center quote exchange rates for all three major currencies. Then, the centers quoting all three currencies can be ranked based on the number of Reuters entries from each center. On this basis there are five major international financial centers (in alphabetical order): Hong Kong, London, New York, Singapore, and Tokyo. Next, there are three middle-sized centers: Sydney, Toronto, and Zurich. Small centers quoting exchange rates for all three major currencies are Chicago, Los Angeles, Melbourne, Oslo, San Francisco, and Wellington, and a group from the Middle East, Abu Dhabi, Bahrain, Dubai, Jeddah, and Kuwait. These were the only centers that had quotes for all three currencies on Reuters during 1989.

The Bank for International Settlements (BIS) reports the following market shares in April 2013 for all market centers with a share of at least 1%: United Kingdom, 40.9; United States, 18.9; Singapore, 5.7; Japan, 5.6; Hong Kong SAR, 4.1; Switzerland, 3.2; France, 2.8; Australia, 2.7; Netherlands, 1.7; Germany, 1.7; Denmark, 1.5; Canada, 1.0.[1]

3.1.3. Cross rates (ignoring spreads)

Hard currencies, such as the EUR, USD, GPB, CHF, and JPY, are very liquid and easy to trade. Of course, all hard currencies are traded vis a vis the USD. But in addition dealers typically quote a cross rate for these currencies. A **cross-rate** is an exchange rate between two currencies, neither of which is the USD. Currencies that have low trading volume and are more difficult to trade are called **exotic currencies**. For exotic currencies that are without an active cross market, cross-rates are calculated

---

[1] Bank for International Settlements (September 2013).

from the standard USD quotes.[1] An example of an exotic currency is the Philippine Peso, PHP. Hence, to exchange one exotic currency for another it is first necessary to trade the first currency for USDs and then use the USDs to purchase the second currency. Traders thus incur two spreads.

Now we explain how to calculate cross rates for two currencies. Suppose that we have quotes vis-a-vis the USD for the currency of the Philippines (PHP) and the currency of South Africa (ZAR):

$$USD/PHP\ 42.98\ \text{and}\ ZAR/USD\ 0.10$$

We seek to compute PHP/ZAR and ZAR/PHP. First note that in equation form:

$$(a)\ 1\ USD = 42.98\ PHP =,\ \text{and}$$

$$(b)\ 1\ ZAR = 0.10\ USD.$$

Multiplying both sides of (b) by 10 gives

$$(b1)\ 10\ ZAR = 1\ USD.$$

Because the right hand side of (a) and the left hand side of (b1) are equal to the same thing, namely 1 USD, they must also be equal to each other, which gives:

$$42.98\ PHP = 10\ ZAR$$

or in standard quote form

$$PHP/ZAR\ 0.2327$$

The reciprocal exchange rate is ZAR/PHP 4.298.

If instead we begin with

$$PHP/USD\ 0.02327\ \text{and}\ USD/ZAR\ 10$$

Then we multiple the PHP/USD quote by $1/0.02327 = 42.97$ to produce

$$42.97\ PHP/USD\ \text{or in standard form}\ USD/PHP\ 42.97$$

Now we have 42.97 PHP = 10 ZAR, which we can solve as before.

---

[1] For cross rates see: http://quotes.reuters.com/.

Finally, if we begin with

PHP/USD 0.02327 and ZAR/USD 0.10

We simply multiply the first quote by 42.97 and the second quote by 10 and then proceed as before.

3.2. Forward transactions

In this section we consider two common transactions involving the future delivery of currencies—foreign exchange swaps and outright forwards. Forward contracts involve an agreement today for the delivery of currency at a time beyond the normal settlement period. Forward maturities of one day, one week, two weeks, and one through twelve months are common although other maturities can be negotiated. Forward rates are quoted with respect to spot rates.

3.2.1. Foreign exchange swaps

Most interbank trading involving delivery beyond the spot settlement time is in the form of foreign exchange swaps (which should not be confused with currency swaps). We have mentioned before that a foreign exchange swap involves two exchanges in one trade. One leg of the swap occurs as a spot trade and the second leg occurs at an agreed upon future date.

Trade 1: Party one receives currency 1 now and pays currency 2 now. Party two receives currency 2 now and pays currency 1 now. At a future date the flow are reversed. Party one pays currency 1 and receives currency 2. Party two pays currency 2 and receives currency 1. We emphasize that all of these exchanges are part of the same foreign exchange swap and are all agree to at the initiation of the trade.

It might be useful to show the cash flows from this swap that a hypothetical bank might be offering to make—but without any numbers. We assume that the duration of the future leg is 1 month. A dealer might offer to makes the following exchanges:

	Trade 1			
	Dealer		Customer	
Now	-SGD	+USD	+SGD	-USD
1 month	+SGD	-USD	-SGD	+USD
Net	0	0	0	0

Note that over the life of this swap the cash flows, ignoring the dealer's charges, exactly offset so that each party is in the same position at the end as they were at the beginning.

Alternately, trade 2: Party one receives currency 1 now and pays currency 2 now. Party two receives currency 2 now and pays currency 1 now. At a future date the flow are reversed. Party one pays currency 1 and receives currency 2. Party two pays currency 2 and receives currency 1. It might be useful to show the cash flows from this swap in a table:

	Trade 2			
	Dealer		Customer	
Now	+SGD	-USD	-SGD	+USD
1 month	-SGD	+USD	+SGD	-USD
Net	0	0	0	0

Note that these cash flows are all in the opposite direction from those in trade 1. Again over the life of this swap the cash flows, ignoring the dealer's charges, exactly offset so that each party is in the same position at the end as they were at the beginning.

Assume that we have one dealer but different customers. Then the dealer might actually enter into both trades 1 and 2 so that we can combine the cash flows at least for the dealer. Since the USD cash flows are always 1 in this example, we can ignore the USD cash flows for now. Moreover, for the dealer all the cash flows over the life of these two swaps cancel out so that at the end the dealer is in exactly the same position as at the beginning. We have:

118 Financial Markets

	Trade 1		Trade 2	
	Dealer	Customer	Dealer	Customer
	SGD cash flows			
Now	-	+	+	-
1 month	+	-	-	+
Net	0	0	0	0

Both customers together are also in the same position. Each customer has had the use of a currency that they presumably needed for one month.

Now let's do an example with numbers. Assume that dealers are quoting:

spot: USD/SGD 1.2557/67
swap points: 10/5

We use the convention that all of the SGD cash flows are at the midpoint of the spot spread, namely, 1.2562. Also since all the USD cash flows are for 1 USD we will ignore them. Now we can simply replicate the above table, but add 1.2562 for each SGD cash flow.

	Trade 1		Trade 2	
	Dealer	Customer	Dealer	Customer
	SGD cash flows			
Now	-1.2562	+1.2562	+1.2562	-1.2562
1 month	+1.2562	-1.2562	-1.2562	+1.2562
Net	0	0	0	0

So far we have assumed that the dealer is willing to enter into these transactions without charge. But obviously we would not expect this to be true. In fact the charge that the dealer makes is indicated by the swap points that we provided above. The rule is

IF THE SWAP POINTS ARE IN DESECNDING ORDER

THEY ARE SUBTRACTED

from the quotes. If they are in ascending order, they are added. We subtract the points from the 1 month SGD cash flows. All of the USD cash flows are for a unit of 1 (or a multiple thereof) so again we will ignore them. The only questions is which cash flow is associated with the 10 (0.0010) and which with the 5 (0.0005). The key is that we know that the dealer will make a profit and the customer will incur a cost. Also, we know that from two swaps the dealer's gain and the customer's cost will be (0.0010 − 0.0005 =) 0.0005. Hence, we have:

	Trade 1		Trade 2	
	Dealer	Customer	Dealer	Customer
	SGD cash flows			
Now	-1.2562	+1.2562	+1.2562	-1.2562
1 mo.	+1.2562	-(1.2562	-(1.2562	+1.2562
	-0.0005	-0.0005)	-0.0010)	-0.0010
Net	-0.0005	0.0005	0.0010	-0.0010

3.2.2. Outright forwards

An **outright forward** is a forward contract entered into on a given date that requires the exchange of two currencies at a future date beyond the normal settlement date. Only one exchange of currency is involved. Outright forward contracts are typically between a bank and its commercial or retail customers. Importers or exporters who have payments maturing or coming due in the future can enter into outright forward contracts with banks to lock in the purchase or sale price of the payment currency.

In addition to showing the spread at which foreign exchange swaps can be carried out, swap or forward points are also used to calculate the outright forward price. If the swap points are in descending order they are subtracted and if they are in ascending order they are added.

Suppose that we have the same quotes given above, namely:

spot: USD/SGD 1.2557/67
swap points: 10/5

Hence, given this spot quote and these swap points the outright forward quote is USD/SGD 1.2547/62. We have subtracted 10 pips from the left hand side and 5 pips from the right hand side.

Another fact that can help in determining whether to add or subtract is to know that the outright forward spread is never smaller than the spot spread. In the rare case that the two swap points are equal then the points should be added and the spread is the same for both the spot quote and the outright forward quote.

The reason that the outright forward spread is not less than the spot spread is that the outright forward is actually two trades combined in one. An outright forward is constructed by taking a foreign exchange swap and offsetting the near leg in the spot market. Thus, both the swap spread and the spot spread are incurred.

Outright forwards are not traded in the interbank market. Instead, as we have just indicated, outright forwards are created using forex swaps and spot trades. To understand how banks create outright forwards, when only foreign exchange swaps are traded in the interbank market, we will continue the previous examples: Recall that the cash flows from the foreign exchange swap are:

	Trade 1		Trade 2	
	Dealer	Customer	Dealer	Customer
		SGD cash flows		
Now	-1.2562	+1.2562	+1.2562	-1.2562
1 mo.	+1.2562	-(1.2562	-(1.2562	+1.2562
	-0.0005	-0.0005)	-0.0010)	-0.0010
Net	-0.0005	0.0005	0.0010	-0.0010

To convert these cash flows into the cash flows for an outright forward, if the customer would receive SGD now, then instead that currency is used to buy USD in the spot market at 1.2567. Alternately, if the customer would pay SGD that payment is offset in the spot market at 1.2557. The revised cash flows are:

	Trade 1		Trade 2	
	Dealer	Customer	Dealer	Customer
		SGD cash flows		
Now	-1.2562	+1.2562	+1.2562	-1.2562
Now	+1.2567	-1.2567	-1.2557	1.2557
1 mo.	+1.2562	-1.2562	-1.2562	1.2562
1 mo.	-0.0005	+0.0005	+0.0010	-0.0010
Net	+1.2562	-1.2562	-1.2547	+1.2547

Note that these are the same cash flows that we obtain by simply subtracting (since the swap points are in descending order) the swap points from the respective spot quote.

4. The time pattern of foreign exchange trading

The foreign exchange market is a 24-hour-a-day market for 6 days a week. Nevertheless, there are daily patterns in trading activity as major financial centers around the world open and close. Also, countries have different holidays and different weekends.[1] Examination of the daily ebb and flow of trading can provide additional understanding of the foreign exchange markets.

In Asia there are two distinct periods of trading, with little trading during the Tokyo lunch hour from 4:00 to 5:30. The patterns for Tokyo, Singapore, Hong Kong, and Australia are each similar to the overall Asian pattern. The fact that Singapore and Australia also follow this pattern, despite differing local times, demonstrates the domination of Tokyo in this market. The European profile is also bimodal (i.e., having two periods of high activity), but much less so than the one for Asia. This may reflect different lunch habits or a more spread out lunch time due to local time differences and the lack of domination of the market by a single European center.

In contrast, New York (and Toronto) traders do not appear to take a lunch break. Alternately, one person suggested that "the market perception is the New Yorkers go to lunch and do not come back." Actually, the practice of not returning after lunch may have a sound motivation. It is well known that traders do not like to carry positions overnight and especially over the weekend. Note that Asian traders who have not closed out their positions at the end of the Asian day can stay late (or leave orders with their branches in Europe) and offset their positions in Europe where trading has begun before the end of the Asian day. Similarly, European traders who have not closed out their positions at the end of the European day can offset their positions in New York where trading is still strong. By an accident of time zones, New Yorkers are trading at the end of the day. And

---

[1] Goodhart and Demos (1991) show these time patterns.

there is very little trading from the 40th half hour of the day until the second half hour of the next day. This is especially serious on weekends when trading will not resume until the following Monday morning in Japan. Consequently, New Yorkers are forced to complete their transactions relatively early in the day, especially on Fridays.

5. Summary

The foreign exchange market is an over-the-counter market which involves the exchange of one currency for another and which handles a daily volume of more than 5 trillion USD. The major participants in foreign exchange markets are banks, brokers, commercial firms, and central banks. There are two types of foreign exchange trades—spot trades and forward trades. In the spot market delivery is normally within one or two business days, depending on the currencies involved. Agreements for delivery beyond the normal spot settlement times are forward transactions.

There are two types of forward transactions—foreign exchange swaps and outright forwards. Most forward transactions in the interbank market are foreign exchange swaps while outright forwards predominate in bank dealings with commercial customers. In a foreign exchange swap two currencies are exchanged now with a subsequent exchange in the reverse direction at an agreed date. An outright forward is an agreement to exchange currencies at a settlement date beyond the spot settlement date. Combining a foreign exchange swap and a spot trade can create outright forwards.

The standard practice is to quote all exchange rates against the USD. An exchange rate between two currencies, neither of which is the USD, is called a cross-rate. For some very active currency pairs, cross rates may be quoted and traded directly. For currencies for which there is no quoted cross rate, a cross rate can be obtained by exchanging one currency for USD and then using the USD to buy the second currency.

Questions

1. Suppose that the volatility of a currency's exchange rate increases. What is likely to happen to the currency's bid-ask spread? Why?

2. Consider the following quotes: CHF/USD 0.80, USD/CHF 1.25. Which is in American terms and which is in European terms? How can you tell?
3. In a Forex swap do prices matter or only swap points?
4. What is the difference between swaps and outright forwards? When would each be used?
5. Consider the following quote: CHF/USD 1.22/1.2241.
    a. Is this quote American or European?
    b. Interpret the bid. Interpret the ask.
    c. If a dealer completes two trades, one at the bid and one at the ask, what is the dealer's gain?

References

Allan, Richard, Rob Elstone, Geoff Lock, and Tom Valentine, 1990, Foreign Exchange Management. (Allen and Unwin, North Sydney, Australia).

Andrews, Michael D., 1984, Recent trends in the U.S. foreign exchange market, Quarterly Review. (Federal Reserve Bank of New York, New York).

Bank for International Settlements, September 2013, Triennial Central Bank Survey: Foreign Exchange Turnover in April 2013: preliminary global results.

Bishop, Paul, 1992, Foreign Exchange Handbook (New York, McGraw-Hill).

Carew, Edna, and Will Slatyer, 1994, FOREX: The Techniques of Foreign Exchange (Heinemann Asia, Singapore).

Goodhart, Charles, and Antonis Demos, 1991, Reuters screen images of the foreign exchange markets: The yen/dollar and the sterling/dollar spot market, Journal of International Securities Markets 5, 35-64.

Madura, Jeff, 1995, International Financial Management, 4th ed. (West, New York).

Luca, Cornelius, 1995, Trading in the Global Currency Markets (Prentice-Hall, Englewood Cliffs, NJ).

Manuell, Guy, 1986, Floating Down Under: Foreign Exchange in Australia (The Law Book Company, North Ryde, Australia).

Walmsley, Julian, 1992, The Foreign Exchange and Money Markets Guide (Wiley and Sons, New York).

www.ingramcontent.com/pod-product-compliance
Lightning Source LLC
Chambersburg PA
CBHW051715170526
45167CB00002B/674